The Beginning . . .

Humanity arrived very late on the scene of life.

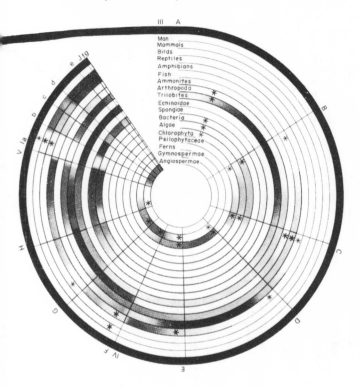

This illustration shows the development of life from the origin of the Earth to the appearance of the first human. Each millimeter corresponds to two million years. The seven inner circles correspond to seven groups of plants; the outer circles to groups of animals. The variations of the shading indicate their evolution, progressive or regressive.

303.49
P33o

124772

Pergamon Titles of Related Interest

Peccei   THE HUMAN QUALITY
Botkin, et al.   NO LIMITS TO LEARNING: Bridging the
Human Gap
de Montbrial   ENERGY: THE COUNTDOWN
Gabor, et al.   BEYOND THE AGE OF WASTE
Giarini   DIALOGUE ON WEALTH AND WELFARE: An
Alternative View of World Capital Formation

One Hundred Pages for the Future

Reflections of the President of The Club of Rome

Aurelio Peccei

Pergamon Press
New York Oxford Toronto Sydney Frankfurt Paris

Pergamon Press Offices:

U.S.A.   Pergamon Press Inc., Maxwell House, Fairview Park,
                     Elmsford, New York 10523, U.S.A.

U.K.   Pergamon Press Ltd., Headington Hill Hall,
                     Oxford OX3 0BW, England

CANADA   Pergamon Press Canada Ltd., Suite 104, 150 Consumers Road,
                     Willowdale, Ontario M2J 1P9, Canada

AUSTRALIA   Pergamon Press (Aust.) Pty. Ltd., P.O. Box 544,
                     Potts Point, NSW 2011, Australia

FRANCE   Pergamon Press SARL, 24 rue des Ecoles,
                     75240 Paris, Cedex 05, France

**FEDERAL REPUBLIC   Pergamon Press GmbH, Hammerweg 6
OF GERMANY**   6242 Kronberg/Taunus, Federal Republic of Germany

303.49
P330
724972
may 1983

Printed in the United States of America

To those who are young
in years or in spirit
— the only hope
for the future of humanity.

Table of Contents

PART II. THE STRAIGHT AND NARROW PATHS TO RENAISSANCE

The Decisive Decade

The Great Hidden Resource

Index of Graphs and Tables

Foreword

I have repeatedly been asked to write a book about the alternatives facing humankind. After some hesitation, I have agreed to do so, for reasons that I think I must explain to the reader since they are the justification for this book.

The human race is hurtling towards disaster. It is absolutely essential to find a way to change course. If a book written with that goal is to be effective, it must have impact — it must be a book to be read in a weekend and pondered over for a year. However, people have very little time to read, and have so many things to do that they don't want to add others. Moreover, having heard many empty words, they no longer believe in promises of a better future. To get people's attention, such a book must be short, honest, and clear; it must point out the dangers that lie ahead, but at the same time convince people that there are possibilities and means of avoiding them.

No doubt this is a task beyond my powers. Nevertheless, I wanted to offer my contribution, however modest, in order to stimulate others to do the same. So I have written this book. It is short. There are about one hundred pages dealing with the future, and with the present from which the future springs; the rest are a link to the past. It is an honest book as well. It describes the reality of the present and the potential of the future as I see them after much thought and discussion. I hope that it is also clear and convincing enough to make the reader think.

I have used simple language, which I understand and which I hope can be understood. To keep the book from being too bulky, I have not tried to exhaust any theme, but have dealt with questions in general outline. I have also kept quotations, statistics, and examples to a minimum. As for the many important questions that I have not touched on, such as energy policy, civil violence and terrorism, and the role of multinational enterprises, I believe my views are implicit in the sense of the total discussion. A society that, in order to survive, adapts its policies to the scale of the individual human being, can only give preference to so-called soft energy paths, especially to solar energy; violence will be basically foreign to such a society; and while granting as much liberty as possible to private enterprises, which are the main economic tool so far devised, society cannot allow them to pursue interests that conflict with the common good. The information revolution, which people talk about so readily, should be less a revolution of *how* we communicate — that is, one of hardware and software — than of *what* we communicate, and it is to the latter end that these pages are devoted.

I have tried to point out the negative factors that are the causes of the present decline that humankind is suffering. And, on the other hand, I have tried to highlight those great, fundamental changes in human thought and behavior that are essential to bring about a new age of renaissance. These changes are the crux of the argument.

The message of this book, in effect, is that *humanity can emerge from this crisis and build almost literally the future it desires*, if it can make intelligent use of its resources, above all its human resources. The decade of the 'eighties will be decisive. The changes that are necessary and possible will demand more than a few sacrifices, but these will be smaller than those that humanity will be forced to make if it continues along its present path.

These are my personal beliefs, not those of The Club of Rome, an informal group in which each member is asked to express his ideas freely even if they differ from those of others, and in which no member may speak in the name of all. The opinions presented here are thus my own but, if a fair number of my colleagues approve of them, I should be happy for this book to become, as have many others, a report to The Club of Rome.

The panorama of humankind that I have traced to this dramatic threshold in its history is consequently my own responsibility, as are all the errors that these pages may contain. It goes without saying, however, that I have gained enormous benefit from my membership in The Club of Rome. I also have drawn upon the works of many other thinkers, researchers, critics, or visionaries who have pondered the human condition. I thank them with all my heart. I hope that someone among them may be able to find, in what I have written, an echo or a confirmation of his or her ideas, or the encouragement to commit himself or herself once more to the cause of humanity.

Finally, I owe a great deal to Anna Maria Pignocchi for her constant and intelligent collaboration.

Aurelio Peccei

Rome, January 1981

Preface To The U.S. Edition

This edition is appearing at a moment when tensions are reaching a climax in human society. No coherent plans or policies are in sight to assure food, energy, shelter, medical care, education, and a decent life to the world's rapidly growing population; and even in the industrial countries the complex political, social, economic, security, and even environmental problems of our time are becoming ever larger and more intractable.

All peoples and nations are responsible for this confused and worsening state of affairs. Everywhere, decision makers in local communities, national governments, and international organizations, as well as in private enterprises and labor unions, are uncertain about what measures should be adopted and unclear about the consequences of their own action or inaction. The United States, the most powerful of all nations, is experimenting with a set of new policies, the results of which can be judged only over the years to come. For the time being, the severe impact of this change on U.S. society and on other countries is just becoming appreciable.

It is difficult to assess how long this somber phase of contemporary history will last, or what its outcome will be. This book tries to show the real nature and depth of the current human crisis, and the dangers that threaten our very survival as a species if the present downward global trends are not halted and reversed. It stresses at the same time that such a redirection is possible, and that it is within our power to steer away from disaster and chart a new course for humankind toward more worthy and "desirable" futures. We possess all the knowledge and means needed to carry out this epochal reorientation of human destiny, but we must learn how to use them intelligently, all peoples and nations together, in a spirit of mutual solidarity, to improve the conditions of life on the planet for the benefit of one and all.

I hope that the message of warning and call for a new sense of responsibility contained in these pages will be well received by the American public, which commands such a decisive influence over the ideas that move the world. If this happens, credit should be given in large part to the meticulous and thoughtful adaptation of the original French text of the book for this U.S. edition by Donald R. Lesh, a colleague to whom I feel greatly indebted for his valued collaboration.

A.P.

New York, September 1981

PART I.
THE ASCENT AND DECLINE OF HUMANKIND

The Future Is No Longer What It Used To Be*

The Future in the Past

Every age has had its burden of misfortunes and dangers and has nurtured its hopes. In past centuries, however, changes came so slowly that, except during periods of calamities, life for the individual, the family, the town, and the countryside was undoubtedly harder than ours, but was quite predictable. One could anticipate that the present and the future would be as like as two drops of water. Craftsmen, merchants, and peasants were constantly pressured by money-lenders, and the taxes due to the prince or the church left people virtually penniless and with little to eat. They knew that their children were likely to die in infancy; that there were wolves and other wild animals in the mountains or far away on the plains; and that thieves regularly swooped out of the forests to attack unescorted travellers. It was normal for wars and famines to rage from time to time.

In the old days, emigration — whether due to foreign invasion, overpopulation, or internal rebellion — led to

---

* Title inspired by Paul Valéry

the establishment of colonies in new worlds reflecting the same values and customs, if not the same institutions, as those of the home country. During the centuries of the great discoveries, the valiant captains and daring adventurers who left to explore and conquer the unknown did no more than add territories to existing kingdoms and empires, imposing their faith and their law on the vanquished peoples. When the explorers returned, their spoils of gold, precious stones, spices, and slaves served merely to enhance the quality of life in the home country.

The evolution of ideas and everyday reality was almost imperceptible; one generation succeeded another without appreciable change. Perhaps it was the boredom of the slow passage of dismal, hard days and long nights, the feeling that today would be no different from yesterday, and that tomorrow and the day after would be the same —in short, the sheer monotony of life — that prompted the need to escape into an imaginary world, to believe in fairy tales and fables and to create myths. The fantastic world of dragons, monsters, sea-serpents, wizards, fairies, and goblins was the prodigious child of this grey and unchanging reality.

If the future was full of mystery, it was because it was shaped by the thought of the life beyond and the unquestioned belief that Hell and Heaven truly existed. The future belonged to God. Mortals would, according to the good or evil deeds of their lifetimes, either be rewarded by the Lord with unsurpassed bliss, or punished for eternity; the soul was all that mattered. And so the human imagination created a host of spirits and deities to take control over mortal life. People believed that the future was a long journey in the kingdom of the dead for which one had to prepare; or that every individual would be reincarnated after death in an endless cycle; or even that a disquieting and boundless nothingness would finally engulf everything and everybody. Minds were turned toward the future much more then than now, but daily life was detached from that transcendental destiny. And life on Earth went on with an almost unchanging rhythm and immutable principles, from one century to another.

The Future in the Present

Modern men and women have abruptly altered the nature of the future and brought it down to their level. Through rigorous and infinitely patient scientific analysis, they have probed the secrets of matter and the forces of the Earth and the Universe. They have demystified the world of fantasy, brought metaphysics under scrutiny in the laboratory, and pushed the frontiers of the unknown far back into the vast infinity of cosmic and galactic space, and the minute infinity of subatomic particles. This does not mean, however, that human beings know themselves any better than before.

In fact, supremely confident in its knowledge of the environment and natural phenomena, the human species is taking liberties with the future. People believe that, with the help of certain data and basic hypotheses, they are now in a position to unveil part of the future, to sketch its outlines in so-called scenarios, or at least to project trends affecting the average individual, or a trade, profession, or industry. They make forecasts of anything and everything and develop countless short- and medium-term projections for many human activities.

Having discovered, however, that there are many risks in

the human future on Earth, people try to find means to control them or at least to protect against them in various ways. They develop remedies for numerous diseases, stockpile wheat, record information on everything of interest, attempt to forecast climate variations, and create welfare systems to guarantee minimal well-being and meet basic needs in times of adversity and in old age.

Meanwhile, in this search for security, human beings have fallen into a trap of their own unwitting creation. Though it is true that they can in part predict the very near future and protect themselves against some of its hazards, their progress in this regard often has an adverse effect in the long term. Intoxicated by their own abilities and immediate successes, they do not realize that they will often have to pay very dearly in the future for the benefits of today. Ultimately, in their total reliance on scientific reasoning, they forget the inspirations of philosophy, ethics, and faith, which alone can give lasting harmony to their endeavors. Without such support, and with too heavy reliance on their technological expertise, people rush headlong down the paths opened by technology without questioning where they may lead. The human future thus becomes totally unpredictable.

Furthermore, as progress is achieved and enterprises expand, human beings must constantly invent more and more complex and sophisticated systems to monitor and manage their activities, whether in urban affairs, industry, information, communications, or transportation. They become so engrossed in this task that they have no time left to worry whether the development of these systems may diminish or damage their relationship with Nature, already greatly impaired although essential for human survival. When Nature does not respond as they wish, men and women of today imagine that they can take its place or even improve on it by hybridizing species or manipulating genes, though they lack the wisdom and patience that Nature has always shown in evolution. No one can foresee what the consequences may be.

Modern human beings are so enmeshed in the intricacies of their various elaborate devices that, in an attempt to maintain control, they turn to new and ever more complex instruments and mechanisms. They try to endow computers — their most exciting achievement, already assisting or virtually replacing humans in all decisions — with the heuristic capabilities of an artificial intelligence. With the aid of computers, they hope to find their way through the maze of their half-natural and half-mechanistic world. They place more and more confidence in mathematical models to simulate the reality of the strange new system they have created, and to discover the logic of its behavior.

It is not surprising that all these efforts have not succeeded in rescuing us from the sea of troubles in which we are now foundering. The reason is that these efforts are inspired by the same mentality that is the cause of the present crisis. We search for paths of progress, comfort, and welfare totally outside ourselves, without considering how to improve what we are, and how we think and act. Modern men and women are able to transform everything else, but they forget to adapt themselves accordingly.

The final result is that the future now appears more precarious and obscure than ever before.

The End of Self-Regulating Mechanisms

These few comments are sufficient to suggest how badly

equipped we are to understand the destiny toward which we are recklessly heading. In the past, some natural mechanisms could have helped us, but now they have become weak and uncertain, and their operation is unreliable.

The regenerative capacity of Nature is one of those self-regulating mechanisms. In its amazing wisdom, acquired by uninterrupted experimentation through the ages, Nature developed self-controlling, self-adjusting, and readjusting devices that exist to a lesser or greater degree in all living organisms. This property, called homeostasis, also gives ecosystems a remarkable ability to absorb, or to reduce and reject, foreign pollutants or abnormalities. All these characteristics nevertheless have limits, and the pressures exerted by modern men and women have transgressed those limits in many areas. The living world can no longer cope with the massive injection of wastes from our industrial civilization and the thousands of new chemical substances that it continuously produces. Nature's regenerative capacity no longer can repair all the damage wrought by humans.

Until quite recently, there were also some reliable self-regulating mechanisms in human systems, but they have also broken down or begun to function erratically. That is the case, for example, with the political institutions of democratic countries. In simpler times, their strength lay in the periodic consultation of the electorate and the alternation of political parties following the discussion of ideas and evaluation of various policies by the citizens. These mechanisms are no longer able to maintain a productive balance that has been put to the test and readjusted frequently over time, which is fundamental to democracy. Even when the mechanisms function normally, they can no longer satisfy the demand for participation and innovation in our complex and integrated societies of today, confronted as they are with problems that neither the parties nor the voters, nor perhaps even the experts, understand. Our age clearly demands new political and social processes better suited to our times, but they remain to be invented.

The balance of supply and demand has suffered a similar fate. Scarcity of a number of resources, anarchy in monetary systems, galloping inflation, politics of monopoly and oligopoly, as well as increasing state intervention at national and international levels have transformed and distorted the adjustment mechanism almost beyond recognition. Prices are often politically set or are largely manipulated and fixed outside the market; they are no longer its result but one of its primary components. On the other hand, buyers, brainwashed by advertising, are no longer free decision-makers. Neither the producer nor the consumer, nor even society itself can any longer trust the "invisible hand" of classical economics, which they believed would guide them all toward an optimum level. Instead, they often find themselves kicked along by a "mysterious boot."

I might cite another example. It has always been assumed that lessons for the future could be drawn from the observation of the past. The study of the historical pattern of changes in human systems was thus thought to help in forecasting future trends. There is an interesting application in the field of economics, which, to be sure, is always accorded the place of honor. Analysis of the historical fluctuations of economic phenomena suggests that they are governed by three distinct kinds of cycles: the first is the normal short-term economic or business cycle (from 3 to 7 years); the second, known as the Kuznets cycle, is medium-term (from 15 to 25 years); the third is very long-term (from

45 to 60 years) and is called the Kondratieff cycle. Among the innumerable current economic forecasts, many rely on such cyclical research.

I do not deny that the analysis of the past may shed some light on the origin of certain phenomena and on the reasons for their variations, and I recognize that the interpretation of cycles may be a useful tool for this analysis. The extrapolation of trends from the past into the future may, however, easily mislead us. We live in a period of fundamental changes that correspond to breaks in past patterns, discontinuities, even reversals of trends. To rely too heavily on the past for our guidance could mean that we venture into the future looking backwards.

The phase of history before us is completely new. The lessons of the past are no longer fully applicable, and the mechanisms that once automatically absorbed and corrected our mistakes have ceased to function. To guide us, we need a radical change in our attitudes, and an effort in innovative imagination that is both courageous and realistic.

Facing the Future Alone

Indeed, we must change because the future is no longer what it used to be. The difference lies in the fact that its relation to the present is essentially new. The future will no longer be a mere *continuation* of the present, but a direct *consequence* of it. Our forefathers, with some reason, could consider the future as an extension of their own time, in the same way that their present was dominated by the same kind of adversities and the same range of alternatives that had characterized their past. Now the differences are profound. The contrast between even the most recent past and the present is obvious; and even though the present is necessarily the starting point for the future, the gap between the two promises to grow even wider. This is because the human being has begun to play a determining role — not only that of protagonist, but also of author of his own history.

The future is clearly not predetermined, as if inscribed in a great, secret book for the prophets or scholars among us to decipher. Nor is the future the accidental product of unknown and hidden forces. Admittedly, extraordinary events such as the appearance of a comet or the vagaries of sun spots may change the conditions of life on Earth. But the stakes are too high to allow this level of speculation to distract us. And we need only a little common sense to reject the view that the future can be determined by benign or malevolent supernatural powers. Our knowledge of the history of the planet and of human beings leads us to search for the logic of the future in a more objective and realistic way.

The future which concerns us, and which this and succeeding generations must depend on, or fear, will be *a product of human choice.* Modern men and women have now become the principal agents of change in this small corner of the Universe under their control. In these circumstances, the future will essentially depend on them, or rather on the daily activities and behavior of the entire world population. If it is the sum total of their disorders, struggles, and pettiness, the future will be miserable and the world unbearable. If, however, it is a responsible creation, the result of a committed effort to improve upon the present, the future will then be worthy of the human quality, and the world a place where people can live, work, and love in peace for generations to come.

It is the first time that humankind is facing the global future alone; the first time that men and women hold the future so completely in their hands, and can plot the course of Spaceship Earth on its voyage toward centuries to come. The responsibilities are both exhilarating and terrifying. As the great biologist Julian Huxley aptly put it, "man's role, whether he wants it or not, is to be the leader of the evolutionary process on Earth, and his job is to guide and direct it in the general direction of improvement." Are we capable of carrying out this extraordinary mission?

The answers that we give are probably less important than the question itself. It certainly leads us to realize that we are in a totally new position, with unprecedented responsibilities, and that we may bring about a disastrous future through our ignorance, carelessness, shortsightedness, or stupidity. It should also make us appreciate the inanity of attempting to predict the future, as many of us are inclined to do, and the urgent necessity instead to devote ourselves intelligently to its creation. Even the most gifted individual is incapable of foreseeing the complexity of all the elements that combine to shape the future. But, together, all human beings can — and must — invent and build the future.

The future is the most important and daunting human invention. As will be seen in the following pages, it can only be a cultural invention, for the future will either be the inspired product of a great cultural revival, or there will be no future.

One Future For All

The new vision of ourselves, our world, and our role

within it must be based on this fundamental concept of human mastery of the global future. For philosophical reasons and practical purposes, this concept must also be qualified by the essential corollary of *the common destiny of humankind.*

The world is continuously — and ever more rapidly —growing smaller in relation to the number, power, and aspirations of its inhabitants. It will inevitably grow more integrated and more interdependent. The interconnections between the various human systems that underpin society will multiply until they form what I will later call the worldwide *metasystem*, the internal dynamics of which will ever more be mutually reinforcing.

To speak of world unity today, therefore, is no longer to express a pious hope, or engage in empty rhetoric; it is purely and simply to recognize an emerging reality that tomorrow will be even stronger and clearer. In 1971, in Menton, more than 2000 scientists from many disciplines embodied this recognition in a moving but unheeded message to the United Nations. They expressed their conviction thus: "Widely separated though we are geographically, with very different cultures, languages, attitudes, political and religious loyalties, we are united in our time by an unprecedented common danger. This danger, of a nature and magnitude never before faced by man, is born of a confluence of several phenomena. Each of them would present us with almost unmanageable problems; together they present not only the probability of vast increases in human suffering in the immediate future, but the possibility of the extinction, or virtual extinction, of human life on Earth. ... Earth, which has seemed so large, must now be seen in its smallness. We live in a closed system, absolutely dependent on Earth and on each other for our lives and those of succeeding generations. The many things that divide us are therefore of infinitely less importance than the interdependence and danger that unite us."

If the world shall be one, so shall its destiny: one single destiny for the great human family, only one for the whole of humankind. Of course, there will always be marked differences between regions in climate, sunlight, rainfall, wildlife, and vegetation; and between nations in their inhabitants' temperaments, customs, and tastes, their inclination to work or meditation, their economic level and outlook on life. Similarly, individual variations and characteristics will always exist in the basic conditions and evolutionary patterns of different societies. The worldwide distribution of the human race and the sheer abundance and variety of cultures demonstrate the remarkable adaptability of the human species, which is an irreplaceable treasure. But this will not prevent all human societies from moving toward the same destiny, whatever their present conditions. Even the superpowers —with their military strength, economic power, and other means of imposing their will — cannot halt that process.

One of the greatest socio-political and economic differences between the future and the present is that the increasingly intertwined structures of the entire global system will produce *a progressive convergence of the futures of all peoples.* All societies will be bound together ever more closely by a network of vital interlinkages, which will condition their relationships with each other for better or for worse. Breaking these links will no longer be conceivable. It would throw the whole system into chaos — which no one would want.

Only the realization that each society has an interest in the progress and welfare of all other societies will open the

laxies, each of which is made up of

ther Earths similar to our own exist
rs, but ours is the only one that directly
about half the age of the Universe.
ealing with its very near future — a few
elp us to understand it better if we take
glance into the unfathomable depths of
that I mentioned at the outset. With this
nparisons easier, let us assume that the
years old. The first manifestations of life
ve appeared about half-way through its
e billion years ago.
ose two dates to the scale of the six-day
o Saturday, in Genesis, Earth would have
e first few minutes of Monday morning.
would have appeared during the first few
rsday morning. Then, slowly but surely,
e fruit and organic life was established in
ersal energy. Life began to be disseminated,
come specialized, and to influence its envi-
biosphere was taking shape. In successive
ething mass of life-forms, becoming ever
, spread during the three days of Thursday,
Saturday and succeeded progressively in
e whole planet.
ut 200 million years ago, this life-chain pro-
st advanced species, the mammals, Saturday
just beginning. Evolution was following its
xorable course. It was only in more recent
ges, however, that our distant ancestors —
, eating insects and fruit — left the forests for
d began to walk upright. Many more million

way to a better future. This is a fundamental principle that must be recognized as soon as possible. We already have made progress in acknowledging the interdependence of ecosystems and recognizing that their individual and collective biological diversity is a factor of strength and stability rather than a weakness. The time has come to realize that our entire metasystem is in an analogous position. We all have an interest not only in our own future, which is obvious, but also in the future of other nations with which, in spite of our differences, we share a common destiny.

These few observations open the way to understanding the urgency of the need for humankind to become better prepared for the future, to improve its moral and existential — in a word, cultural — qualities. The future is no longer what it was thought to be, or what it might have been if humans had known how to use their brains and their opportunities more effectively. But the future can still become what we reasonably and realistically want, provided we sincerely want it and have the determination to improve ourselves.

We have reached a point in the human adventure at which a combination of knowledge, power, and will may still give us the keys to the future. It is up to us to learn to use them wisely and well.

Ma

number of other g
billions of stars.

Very probably o
among all these sta
interests us. It is
Although we are d
decades — it will l
that retrospective
the preceding eras
aim, to make cor
Earth is six billior
are thought to ha
existence, or thre

To gain a s
the depths of
us to see the t
ously at the sur
marginal positi
dous distance is
these two positi
embarking on he
approximations.
only as a challen
perspective will pro
edgeable readers w
where necessary.

It is said that the
years ago, apparently
primary energy. In or
world, a heavenly boo
pared with the whole U
ual planet in the solar s
in the cosmos as part of

If we relate th
week, Monday t
been born in th
The seeds of life
minutes of Thu
those seeds bor
the flux of univ
to evolve, to be
ronment. The
stages, this se
more complex
Friday, and
enveloping th

When, abo
duced its mo
evening was
slow but ine
geological a
tree-dweller
the plains a

years had to elapse before some species of advanced anthropoids — in the process of hominization — appeared here and there on Earth. These were our direct progenitors, and the date of their presence can be put at about ten million years ago, which corresponds to fifteen minutes before midnight on Saturday. Their brain was already fairly well developed, their erect gait had left their arms and hands free, and they could already grasp objects. It was from these primates that our species finally emerged a million years ago.

The week in Genesis ended on Saturday on the stroke of midnight and *the human adventure began.* All that preceded it may have been merely a prelude to the entry of human beings on the scene — but what an awe-inspiring prelude! The diagram at the beginning of the book gives us an extremely comprehensive and probably very rough idea of the evolution of life. Nevertheless, I feel that even a quick look at it counsels us to regard ourselves with humility, and reminds us how petty it is to limit the horizons of our future to a few years, or even to a few decades.

Barely a Million Years of Human Life

With the appearance of the human species about a million years ago, a new era began. In relation to our cosmological reference calendar, its duration up to now corresponds to less than a minute. The whole of the human adventure has taken place within this tiny span of time, and yet it has completely upset the rhythm of life on Earth.

Was it then in a burst of creativity, or in a moment of folly, that Nature produced the last great species, which we have called *Homo sapiens?* Are we Nature's masterpiece or,

on the contrary, a misfit that escaped the triage of immediate selection and was thrust into the maelstrom of life for
a later judgment? And will Nature finally eliminate
humans if they come in conflict with too many other
species or become biologically weak? These questions are
highly controversial, and will be discussed below. I propose that, for the time being, we pronounce a favorable
verdict on humanity, while remembering that, in relation
to the gradual cycles of evolution, a million years is probably too short a period to justify a final conclusion.

In order to understand what is happening to our species
now, and what might happen to it tomorrow, we must
examine this million years of human existence more
closely. For this purpose, we must adopt a different scale
and a different calendar — the more familiar scale of
centuries and the calendar of human history.

A million years is ten thousand centuries. From the very
beginning, the human race had to struggle hard in a world
that was already filled by millions of other species. First,
we gradually had to win our own place in the habitat that
we shared with so many others; then, we progressively had
to assure our position in the competition for food and
security. However, the unique assets of our brain and
hands — and the tools, shelters, and weapons that they
enabled us to construct — soon gave us absolute superiority over all competitors. Finally, with the more advanced
articulation of speech, which in turn stimulated our intelligence and memory, and with the added advantage of our
ability to organize ourselves into communities, we became
invincible.

We must recognize, however, that we know very little of
the struggles and vicissitudes that marked our ascent, and
of the thoughts and customs that we had developed during

the whole prehistoric period, that is, for 99 percent of the ten thousand centuries of human existence. The best-known part of our extraordinary experience begins, by and large, only ten thousand years, or one hundred centuries, ago. These are *the hundred centuries that count*. They correspond to one percent of the human era, and to half a second on the time scale of Genesis.

Indeed, a new chapter opened at the moment when, having discovered or invented the first rudimentary techniques of cultivating the land, humans ceased being simply hunters and gatherers of fruit and also became tillers of the soil. Our place in nature rapidly changed. To feed ourselves, we no longer needed to keep vast expanses of land under our control so that we could live on the wild animals and plants that existed there. Now we could satisfy our needs by cultivating smaller areas. Human life had become more secure; vaster horizons were opening before us.

The Hundred Centuries That Count

The invention, which was also a discovery, of agriculture, like the discovery of fire that had preceded it, precipitated all kinds of far-reaching changes in the human condition — as well as a fair number in that of many other forms of life everywhere on the planet. For our species, the advent of agriculture also represented *a cultural metamorphosis*, the greatest one until now. At that time, the human race was made up of small family or tribal communities, in any case not more than a few million individuals in all. We gradually settled on fertile lands, and began to expand demographically as well as culturally.

With greater security and more free time, men and

women were no longer obliged to concentrate all their efforts on survival. Now our forebears could also satisfy less pressing needs, make their existence more pleasant, and record its most outstanding events. Reliable indications, ever more abundant and precise, of their thoughts, their ways of expression, and their patterns of life have come down to us. Thus began —about one hundred centuries ago — what we call *the Historical Period.* As we have seen, one hundred centuries is an extremely brief period of time compared to the cycles of evolution. But it was all that our ancestors needed to elevate their minds and spirits to the heights of artistic expression, their social imagination to the flowering of glorious civilizations, their military and civic qualities to the founding of great empires, and to make conquests and discoveries which, as used to be said, made them rulers of the earthly domain.

However, this cursory overview of the epic human story will not give us the real sense of our past unless we pay special attention to two periods — both of outstanding importance, albeit of contrary significance to one another.

The first period in human history that is particularly worthy of note is that of *the birth of the great religions.* It occupies roughly a quarter of those hundred centuries, coming between the second millennium before Christ and the advent of Islam in the middle of the 7th century A.D. These great spiritual movements have survived all kinds of upheavals and still have a deep, although no longer decisive, influence on the life of our technological societies. Yet they were conceived in essentially rural or nomadic societies, when men and women lived in direct and permanent contact with Nature.

Nature and the mystery of its creation had always seized the human imagination. Gazing upon the vastness of the seas, the skies, and the Earth itself, we had always wondered what lay beyond that which we could see. Astounded by the different varieties of animals and plants around us, and by their instincts and prodigious capacity to reproduce and survive, we were curious about other non-human beings that might exist elsewhere. Confronted with the fury of storms, winds, seas, volcanoes, earthquakes, and forest fires, we human beings realized that we were indeed insignificant. We had always bowed before Nature's endless marvels and, as our admiration grew, God's existence and His works came to occupy a dominant position in the human mind. The revelation or the intuition of forces immensely greater than ourselves were still inspired by Nature, but now went beyond it. And we became possessed by the need to order our beliefs and feelings.

With the birth and development of the great religions, gradually accepted by the vast majority of human beings, one might have thought that spiritual values from then on would have held our aggressive and materialistic human impulses in check. Having attained inner harmony, we should have been more tolerant and understanding towards our fellows; and, at the same time, we should have become more respectful of the rights of other creatures, in relation to which we held a place of honor on Earth, but not the right of life and death.

But it was not to be so. I do not claim to be an expert, and speak simply as an observer of the world, but I think I may be allowed to say that the blame can be placed in large measure on the recognized representatives or interpreters of those great religions. Their exclusivity has too often gone beyond the declaration or practice of their faith. It has taken the form of a reciprocal intolerance; has stimulated a stubborn adherence to dogma fed by an assertion of religious supremacy, which is the counterpart of national sovereignty; and has sharpened the proselytizing spirit beyond the search for the common good. Theological battles have been transformed into holy wars.

The institutionalization of faith, with the creation of a corps of religious professionals, has not always had happy results. In spite of the sincere vocation and noble inspiration of the great majority of men and women who have devoted themselves to religion, caste consciousness has arisen; more than one church has been partially transformed into a bureaucratic machine with political overtones, and with a tendency to yield to authoritarian temptations. Certain points of doctrine, often formal, have been magnified, provoking schisms, apostasy, and the denunciation of what are claimed to be heresies. The official truth, proclaimed by the initiated as sacred for the mass of believers thirsting for simple, understandable truths within their grasp, has become impossible to question; and, in order that it never should be questioned, ignorance and even superstitions have occasionally been encouraged.

These structural inflexibilities and doctrinal introversions have helped to keep the major religions static even when the winds of change blowing through society have made clear the need to move from one cultural epoch to another. As a result, it is difficult even for their most sensitive and profound theologians and scholars to break out of a system frozen into formulations reflecting the past, a system that cannot adapt itself or its doctrines to modern life. Instead of serving as the courageous vanguard of new ideas as they did in former times, able to comfort, enlighten, and guide people of all conditions, religions now run the risk of becoming a timid rearguard, detached from the problems and aspirations of a bewildered and troubled humanity.

And yet humanity, although the prisoner of materialistic motivations, has a *profound need for spirituality*. It is a visceral need. We humans feel that we are living in a dangerous void, that we must restore communion with spheres that transcend those motivations. The anguish within the churches, the call for a new ecumenism to free them from their narrow confines, the widespread interest in minor cults (which are proliferating, however strange they may be), and a return to a respect for Nature — an ecological respect this time — are all symptoms of this need.

They are encouraging symptoms. For, *without a sincere spiritual awakening, the renaissance of our true humanity will be impossible.*

The Age of the Great Revolutions

The second outstanding, indeed completely exceptional, period in human history is much shorter — from the middle of the 18th century to the present day. Yet it has the character and force of a great earthquake. After a long period of calm, the world burst forth with restless energy.

Two political revolutions, the American and the French, had set society in motion and encouraged bold innovations. Under the combined impacts of the freeing of science from classical dogmas, the rise of the bourgeoisie, the birth of a manufacturing capitalist class, and the use of ever more powerful and more efficient productive machines, what I term *the material revolutions* sprang into life. Industrial and scientific at the outset, this wave of revolutions finally became technological. The latter reached full flood when humans began methodically to apply in practice, on an industrial scale, the knowledge of the physical world that their astonishing scientific progress had created.

On this basis, humanity arrived at the greatest, perhaps the decisive, turning point in its history. The human condition was suddenly changed. *Human beings acquired phenomenal power*, which surpassed their knowledge as well as their capacity to control it and to control themselves.

We have altered the very basis of human life, but we are unable to evolve in harmony with our times. From prehistoric days, people found it necessary to group together according to natural affinities, and to constitute themselves socially and politically into clans, hordes, or tribes, which eventually led to so-called "modern" nations. In order to organize and exploit their domains, these *societies* in turn created *systems* of administrative structures and networks for service, trade, and communication. Societies and systems evolved more or less in parallel. At the present time, however, human societies and human systems have taken divergent paths. On one hand, each society, jealous of its territory and its frontiers, is attempting to conserve its traditions, its customs, its cultural identity, and its independence and political institutions, even to magnify them. On the other hand, all the systems of these societies are expanding, superimposing themselves and encroaching more and more on each other, across all frontiers. The combined pressures of the material revolutions are only serving to accelerate this trend.

Quite recently, in the space of two or three decades — a mere twinkling of an eye by history's clock — the revolutions of our age have themselves undergone a revolution owing to the appearance of high technologies and the extension of large artificial systems. Extremely complex systems now dominate the global scene — in aeronautics and astronautics, defense, manufacturing, energy, transport, agriculture, cybernetics, communications, and data processing. They have radically transformed our daily life. The interdependence to which I frequently allude, and which today has become a familiar term, is the mutual dependence of all these interlinked systems on a national, international, and even global level. It is the functional interdependence of this group of systems that turns them into a super-system — *the global metasystem.*

On the wings of the material revolutions, human beings have experienced a meteoric rise and have crowned themselves absolute masters of the Earth. But our social and political organization is far from having undergone an equivalent evolution. Human society has remained divided into separate, inward-looking units. Each one seeks to go its own way and affirms its independence and its superiority, even its supremacy, at the expense of the others. There may be a global metasystem, but *there is no organic world community* that draws its strength, as in Nature, from the dynamic balance of its many different components. This dichotomy between socio-political development and the structure of technological progress is one of the principal destabilizing factors for humankind at the present time.

The new age, of which we are still only witnessing the dawn, was heralded with heady promises. But it is also filled with other elements that are so unprecedented that their impact cannot yet be defined. In the following chapters, I shall review some of them and endeavor to interpret what their probable effects may be. In this analysis, I shall always take *the human being as the touchstone and point of reference*. For this reason, I shall come back to the individual time and again —for, in the end, everything depends on the human quality.

For the moment, it must be noted that humanity has succumbed to the charms of the material revolutions. In our plans and dreams, we no longer draw inspiration from Nature or the teachings of the prophets, but from the power with which these revolutionary forces have endowed us. The material revolutions have become our new religion, and we carry them to extremes. Moving from the mechanistic world, we have raised our eyes to other horizons, artificial horizons.

Exulting in our own power, and insatiable in our appetites, we admit no opposition. Everything belongs to us. Having already taken possession of the whole planet, we set out to conquer its surroundings. We assert ourselves, exploit, manipulate, decimate, annihilate, not realizing that in so doing we are changing the very essence of things around us. We poison the air and the water on which our very lives depend; we build monstrous cities that keep us prisoners; and we construct the bomb that can put an end to everything. Our exploits have the force of a final paroxysm. They are stages in a race without precedent. But is this a triumphal race, or a mad one? And how much longer can it go on?

Many other troubling questions come to mind. It is obvious that the material revolutions have thrown modern men and women off balance. We lack the maturity, the discipline, the wisdom, and the good sense to make beneficial use of our new power. For a species such as ours, whose essential biological strength is its cerebral power and whose very existence depends upon its cultural capacities, such a disequilibrium can be fatal. We run the mortal risk of being doomed by our own excess of power.

If the current ways in which we wield power truly reflect our inner nature, we may wonder whether, even in the unsophisticated and mystic ages of the past, there were not already in us the seeds of an unbridled ambition and the foreknowledge of a tragic imperial destiny. We may also ask whether it was perhaps to justify our immense aspirations in our own eyes that we were led to conceive God, and thus to attain the privilege — alone among all forms of life — of entering into communion with Him; and even to go so far as to assert that the Almighty had chosen to create us in His own image. Is not this anthropomorphism of the Creator, which is not exclusive to the Christian faith, in reality a form of deification of man?

These questions give rise to others. Indeed, if — before turning to a consideration of the future — we reflect on the past and the present, and try to understand the essence of our humanity and the meaning of the voyage of our species through the whirlwind of life, we may find ourselves still more perplexed. Even if we admit the possibility that this whirlwind has evolved by chance or necessity, it still seems to be guided by certain basic rules and constants. The human species, on the contrary, seems to obey no rule in its present upward surge. As we shall see later, humankind is now moving in a direction contrary to that normally followed by evolution.

We have already asked ourselves whether, all things considered, *Homo sapiens* does not represent a deviant phenomenon in the majestic flow of evolution, whether humankind is not just a quirk of Nature, an ambitious attempt that failed, an error in workmanship, which in time will be cancelled out or absorbed by the adjustments that assure the continual renewal of life. This is a train of thought to be pursued.

The Cancerous Growth of Population

Another form of aberrant behavior of our species deserves serious indictment before the tribunal of life — our exponential population growth, which can only be described as cancerous. Apart from insects, few species multiply so fiercely and blindly as does ours. Moreover, we have shown ourselves to be voracious and insatiable, far beyond our physiological needs, and devoid of any real sense of the need to preserve our habitat. These failings have led the human species to the rapid destruction of immense amounts of the Earth's vital biosphere, thus eroding the very bases of its existence.

Quite recently, a new interpretation has been offered for the disappearance of the Mayan civilization, which had flourished for 17 centuries in what are now the rain forests of Central America until its sudden and inexplicable collapse around 800 A.D. The present theory is that, as their population grew progressively larger, the Mayas cut down the forests in vast areas around their villages. Within a few decades, the denuded soil was washed away by heavy tropical rains, and the population was deprived of its agricultural support.

Many other examples of ecological death are known, brought about by excessive deforestation, super-intensive animal husbandry, or ill-conceived irrigation. The Sahara is a graveyard of civilizations that have contributed in this way to their own demise. Nomads have played a role in turning large areas of Asia into deserts. And if it is difficult to discern in other places whether the desert is more a result of climate change or a product of human activity, we can readily state that uncontrolled population growth often leads to an irreversible retreat on the part of Nature.

It is in the recent past, however, that *the phenomenon of population growth has become pathological.* At the beginning of the Christian era, there were perhaps only 200 or 300 million human beings scattered around the world. From then on, the human family grew constantly, but very slowly, and even suffered a marked decline when bubonic plague ravished Europe in the 14th century. We are not sure of the facts, but it seems that, around the time of the discovery of America, there were probably fewer than 500 million members of this family; by the middle of the 18th century, some 700 million; and, after the French Revolution, human numbers already were approaching 900 million. The rate of increase was accelerating. The first billion was probably reached about 1830. A little less than 100 years was needed to attain the second billion in 1925. Within scarcely 37 years, in 1962, another billion was added, and it took only 13 years to hit the four-billion mark in 1975. By 1980, the total world population was about 4.5 billion.

Fertility is on the wane almost everywhere. But, since the decreasing rate of growth is applied to an ever larger base, the population of the world is still growing at an increasing annual pace. Each minute adds its quota, as the table on page 32 indicates. The current median projections tell us that the Earth will have 6.3 billion inhabitants by the year 2000, and that human numbers will continue to increase for a major part of the next century. The composite diagram on pages 34 and 35 gives an idea of the way in which humankind has grown and will further multiply through the end of the century, while the accelerating speeds

One Minute Of The
Population Explosion

In the next 60 seconds:
- 233 babies will be born
- 26 of these 233 will die before age 1
- 34 more will die before age 15
  - 50 to 75 percent of these deaths can be attributed to a combination of malnutrition and infectious diseases
  - Many who do survive beyond age 15 will be stunted in growth and will suffer brain damage than can incapacitate them for life

*Adapted from *Overcoming World Hunger: The Challenge Ahead,* Report of the Presidential Commission on World Hunger, Washington, D.C., March 1980.

of transport and communications have gone on virtually shrinking the globe. Even though the scales used to represent different phenomena are not the same, a quick glance at the diagram is enough for us to understand that the human race is rushing toward destructive events similar to those that in physics are called "implosions."

To get a better grasp of the dramatic character of the phenomenon of population growth, let us look at *what is happening in the course of this century.* We know that in historical perspective a century is only a tiny span of time

— one hundredth of a hundredth of humanity's ten thousand centuries on Earth. In relation to the age of a person 75 years old, that period would correspond to a little less than three days of life. And yet, in such a short time, spectacular changes have taken place in the world's population, and others even more incredible are on the way.

By 1900, there were about 1.6 billion people in the world. This was a record population, reached by gradual increases over the 9,999 preceding centuries. Subsequently, thanks to progress in medicine, sanitation, and nutrition, infant mortality continued to diminish and the average life expectancy to increase, but there were no moral, social, or economic restraints acting to reduce the birthrate. People could not yet comprehend the problems that were being created, and wherever demographic policies existed, they were invariably pro-natalist. The inevitable consequence was that population growth, completely out of control, leaped to totally unforeseen levels.

It is with the greatest anxiety that we have almost suddenly become aware of the fact that, during the first 80 years of this century, the inhabitants of the world have almost trebled in number. But more frightening are the projections for the remaining 20 years. The demographers forecast that, in just two decades, *a "supplementary" population of almost two billion* — far greater than that attained during all preceding eras — will be added to the already excessive numbers of today.

It is impossible to deny that Paul Ehrlich, the scientist and humanist, is right when he says that *a human bomb is threatening the planet.* The diagrams on page 37 and page 38 show two aspects of this problem in graphic form. One shows the "population mushroom." The other compares population profiles, and indicates how serious

Shrinking Of Our Planet By Man's Increased Tr

YEAR	500,000 BC	20,000 BC	500 BC	300 BC	
Required time to travel around the globe	A few hundred thousand years	A few thousand years	A few hundred years	A few tens of years	
Means of transportation	Human on foot (over, ice bridges)	On foot and by canoe	Canoe with small sail or paddles or relays of runners	Large sail boats with oars, pack animals, and horse chariots	Big (wi hor coc
Distance per day (land)	15 miles	15 - 20 miles	20 miles	15 - 25 miles	20
Distance per day (sea or air)		20 by sea	40 miles by sea	135 miles by sea	175
Potential state size	None	A small valley in the vicinity of a small lake	Small part of a continent	Large area of a continent with coastal colonies	Grea tine oceo

Communica- tions					
Word of mouth, drums, smoke, relay runners, and hand printed manuscripts prior to 1441 A.D.	① The Gutenberg 1441 printing press	② The rapid print Web 1863 newspaper press	③ The Bell 1876 telephone	④ T 1895	

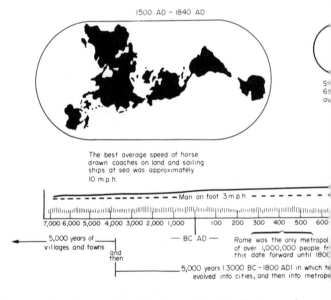

1500 AD – 1840 AD

The best average speed of horse drawn coaches on land and sailing ships at sea was approximately 10 m.p.h.

– – – – – – – – – Man on foot 3 m.p.h – – – – – –

7,000 6,000 5,000 4,000 3,000 2,000 1,000 | 100 200 300 400 500 600

5,000 years of villages and towns *and then*

— BC AD —

Rome was the only metropol of over 1,000,000 people fr this date forward until 1800

5,000 years (3000 BC – 1800 AD) in which te evolved into cities, and then into metrope

Source: Center for Integrative Studies, *World Facts and Trends,* John and Magda McHale, Second Edition, 1972, (updated October, 1980)

nd Communication Speeds Around The Globe

	1900 AD	1925	1950	1980
	A few months	A few weeks	A few days	A few hours
s, , and	Steam boats and railroads (Suez and Panama canals)	Steamships, transcontinental railways, autos, and airplanes	Steamships, railways, auto jet and rocket air-craft	Nuclear-powered ships, supersonic transport 1,450 miles / hour , high speed railway
s	Rail 300-900 miles	400 - 900 miles	Rail 500 -1,500	Rail 1000 - 2000
sea	250 miles by sea	3,000 -6000 air	6000-9500 air	408,000 air
a con- ns -	Large parts of a continent with transoceanic colonies	Full continents and Transocean Commonwealths	The Globe	The Globe and more

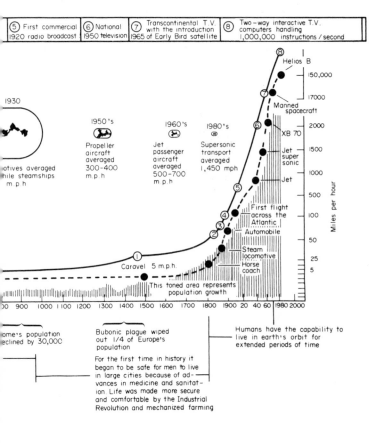

⑤ First commercial 1920 radio broadcast   ⑥ National 1950 television   ⑦ Transcontinental T.V. with the introduction 1965 of Early Bird satellite   ⑧ Two-way interactive T.V. computers handling 1,000,000 instructions / second

⑧ Helios B — 150,000 — 17000 Manned spacecraft

1930

1950's Propeller aircraft averaged 300-400 m.p.h

1960's Jet passenger aircraft averaged 500-700 m.p.h

1980's Supersonic transport averaged 1,450 mph

XB 70 — 2000
Jet super sonic — 1500
Jet — 1000
— 500
First flight across the Atlantic — 100
Automobile — 50
Steam locomotive — 25
Horse coach — 5

Caravel 5 m.p.h.

otives averaged hile steamships m.p.h

This toned area represents population growth

Miles per hour

00 900 1000 1100 1200 1300 1400 1500 1600 1700 1800 1900 20 40 60 1980 2000

ome's population eclined by 30,000

Bubonic plague wiped out 1/4 of Europe's population

For the first time in history it began to be safe for men to live in large cities because of ad-vances in medicine and sanitat-ion. Life was made more secure and comfortable by the Industrial Revolution and mechanized farming

Humans have the capability to live in earth's orbit for extended periods of time

will be the predicted divergence by the year 2000 between
the industrial countries, with a stabilized and aging population, and the young and prolific Third World. After the
end of this century, the gap is destined to grow even wider,
since the great number of men and women of reproductive
age in the less developed countries will vigorously maintain
the high rate of demographic growth there.

I confess that I find it difficult to believe these projections. The speculations of demographers who foresee that
the world's population will become stabilized at around 10
to 12 billion towards the middle of the next century are
purely theoretical. And the calculations of the economists
that show that our good Earth can feed them adequately —
just feed! —simply fail to recognize the realities of life. The
human race is undergoing an explosive phase of growth,
which the biologists tell us occurs when "organisms" find
an abundance of resources and a relative absence of diseases and predators. Such a growth phase is invariably
followed by a phase of rapid contraction, which reduces
their numbers to the size their environment can normally
sustain. It stands to reason, of course, that human beings
are not just mere "organisms." All the same, our demographic explosion is already causing serious instability in the
global system, and will lead to even more grave imbalances
— probably before, not after, the end of the century.

According to the projections cited, by the year 2000 the
population of the Third World will reach 5 billion, while at
present the Third World finds it impossible to feed half
that number decently; and eight countries alone — China,
India, Indonesia, Brazil, Bangladesh, Pakistan, Nigeria,
and Mexico —will contain almost 60 percent of the total
world population. I have the feeling that *well before any
such levels are reached, a chain of crises will be ignited*

The Population Mushroom

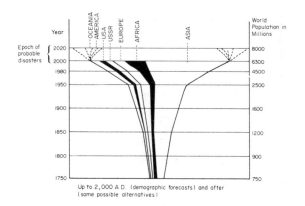

Up to 2,000 A.D. (demographic forecasts) and after
(some possible alternatives)

We can only speculate on what the world population may be after it has reached certain levels. The forecast of six billion around the end of the century suggests an already extremely high level. If human beings do not become Spartan sages or ant-men — beyond the six billion level we will enter the zone of probable catastrophe. The dotted lines show various alternatives at that point. If the population continues to increase, the catastrophe will come later, but will be of a greater magnitude. A sudden population decrease indicates that a catastrophe has already occurred. In any case, pity future generations! If the present generation is not capable of slowing down the birthrate before reaching a total of six billion inhabitants (an arbitrary figure), it will be condemning its successors to inevitable disaster.

Adapted from *Facts and Trends*, prepared by the Center for Integrative Studies, 1979, (c) Magda McHale.

Contrasting Population Profiles

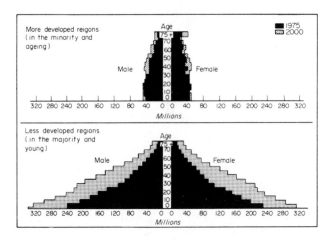

The gap dividing the world into two large groups will inevitably widen further. The differences in age, in number, and structure of the population leave no doubt that tensions in the world will increase.

Source: *The Global 2000 Report to the President*, Study Director, Gerald O. Barney, U.S. Government Printing Office, Washington, D.C., 1980.

somewhere. These will probably be set off in the Fourth World, comprised of the nations of the poorest of the poor. There, or somewhere else, young people will rise in revolt, refusing to accept a fate of hopeless poverty while people in the developed countries continue to live in comparative affluence. One need not be a prophet to imagine that events of this kind will come to pass; that they will trigger off complex and violent crises in which the most modern weapons will be employed — weapons that the industrial nations supply to the poor countries to use them as tools in their power struggles; and finally, that these crises will spread from one region to another like wildfire.

Furthermore, an endemic state of crisis will be fostered in the years to come by *the greatest migration in history*. There can be no doubt that this will be an exodus of the underprivileged, and that it will occur principally in the South of the planet. The movement is already under way. The great majority of the world's inhabitants has always been of peasant origin; it still is, but swelling floods of people are leaving the poor rural areas in search of a less poverty-stricken existence in towns, which appear more attractive but which will ultimately be even poorer and more impossible to live in. On this basis, it is estimated that, in about twenty years' time, the world's population will be divided almost equally between the country and the city.

In certain cases, urbanization will reach almost overwhelming proportions, at the extreme producing monstrous urban concentrations with a projected population equal to that of California. Out of 25 vast urban complexes with more than 10 million inhabitants, 20 will be in the Third World, as may be seen in the table on page 40.

Once again, however, I doubt whether these forecasts

The Megalopolises of the Year 2000

Twenty-five cities will have over ten million inhabitants by the turn of the century. How can we live with such numbers within our limited urban space? Extensive preparations must be made to accommodate this increase in human beings.

	Population in Millions		Population in Millions
Mexico City	31.0	Cairo	13.1
Sao Paulo	25.8	Madras	12.9
Tokyo-Yokohama	24.2	Manila	12.3
New York (with North-eastern New Jersey)	22.8	Buenos Aires	12.1
Shanghai	22.7	Bangkok-Thon Buri	11.9
Beijing	19.9	Karachi	11.8
Rio de Janeiro	19.0	Delhi	11.7
Bombay	17.1	Bogota	11.7
Calcutta	16.7	Paris	11.3
Jakarta	16.6	Teheran	11.3
Seoul	14.2	Istanbul	11.2
Los Angeles-Long Beach	14.2	Baghdad	11.1
		Osaka-Kobe	11.1

United Nations Fund for Population Activities: document prepared for the International Conference on Population and Urban Future, Rome, September 1-4, 1980.

can be correct. I cannot imagine how such concentrations of humanity could possibly exist without either exploding or breaking down. But, if they are actually to exist, their practical problems of food supply, waste disposal, sanitation, police, etc., not to mention their socio-political problems and those of human relationships, seem to me absolutely insoluble. These would no longer be cities, but nightmares.

All these facts and observations give us a glimpse of the future that awaits us if humanity continues its present course of headlong expansion. The picture is fated to become still darker. Unless a miracle or a catastrophe comes to pass, these pathological phenomena of exponential demographic growth will not magically cease in the year 2000. On the contrary, they are likely to continue during part of next century, making the human condition ever more difficult.

But the analysis of our growth problems unfortunately cannot be left with these gloomy considerations. The gravity of the situation does not lie only in the fact that the numbers of people in the world are increasing so rapidly that they will grow fourfold in the course of our century. It also derives from the fact that this demographic explosion is combined with *the explosion of individual consumption and demand.* "The revolution of rising expectations" has been translated into a formidable increase in demand for products, services, and welfare in all countries, whether they are developed, underdeveloped, or overdeveloped. All available means have been employed in an attempt to satisfy this torrent of demands; and, even though the effort has not been completely successful, it has led to unbridled exploitation of natural resources — of minerals, oil, and forests, of water and wildlife, and of agricultural lands, pastures, and fisheries.

The result of the combined dynamics of population growth and consumer demand is that human pressure on natural systems has skyrocketed. Some time ago, I estimated, on the basis of the expected increase in global requirements for metals and industrial raw materials, that this pressure is going to grow by about 70 times during this century, thus imposing a truly crushing burden on our small planet, as can be seen from the diagram on page 43. If, owing to the constraints on economic growth that we are continually discovering, we choose to be more prudent, one might suppose that in the course of the century material consumption will increase only 40 times instead of 70. The result would be appalling, all the same, since the demands on Earth of its approximately 6 billion inhabitants of the year 2000 would be equivalent to that of *more than 60 billion consumers of the year 1900!* Can the Earth support such a heavy burden? And at what cost, in terms of quality of life, for the people of the year 2000 and beyond? What then shall be the heritage that, with our lack of restraint, we leave to succeeding generations? I hope that among my readers there is someone who will revise these figures and try to answer these questions.

An even more frightening assessment — which also needs to be verified — has been made by several inquiring minds. They have calculated that, since the appearance of *Homo sapiens*, about 70 billion human beings have lived on this planet. If this estimate is anywhere near reality, we can deduce that the present population of 4.5 billion represents more than 6 percent of all the human beings that have ever existed. And, supposing that modern men and women on the average live twice as long as their ancestors, and consume ten times more natural resources each year — these two hypotheses being rather conservative — we reach

Increasing Demographic Pressure in the 20th Century

An estimate based on the expected increases in world population and in the industrial consumption of metals and raw materials per capita.

Source: Illustration from the journal *Successo*, Milan, June 1970, for the article "The Predicament of Mankind" by the author.

an astonishing conclusion. This is that the present inhabitants of the Earth will consume, during their lifetimes, *more natural resources than all their ancestors have consumed in the 10,000 preceding centuries*. Others have estimated that, in the last 25 years of this century, our demands for energy will be the equivalent of all the energy consumed during all preceding human history.

Surely the world has never before harbored such creatures. It is enough to make us ask ourselves whether we have not unknowingly become a generation of monsters.

Doubts About Ourselves

At this point, it is appropriate to return to the discussion of the human race. As we are now in the 'eighties — a great turning point in history — we must necessarily give thought to ourselves, our condition, our fate, and to what we must do. Have our technical skills placed us on too high a pedestal? Are we a species of geniuses destined in the long run to triumph over everything? Or, on the contrary, as I have just speculated, have we not been transformed into monsters, monsters who may perhaps have qualities of genius, but who will ultimately fall victim to their own evil deeds?

In view of the great chaos we have created, the thesis that we are geniuses is difficult to defend. On the contrary, the opposing thesis, that we are bio-physically deranged, cannot be so easily rejected. Many would support that view, believing that *our very human nature will act against us*. Our aggressive, cruel, intolerant character, they maintain, has been wonderfully useful to us in imposing our will on other species in the struggle for existence, and has helped us to subjugate our weaker fellows, or exterminate them, without any biological reason, in tribal or religious conflicts. Henceforth, that character will drive us to use our new power to scorch the earth around us — until we eventually bring about our own destruction.

This character is said to be a part of our genetic code, and therefore impossible to change in the short term. It would condemn us to continue our bloody imperial epic, not pausing even in the face of the ultimate consequences. In other words, we would have no chance of escaping from the yoke of our unique intelligence, which either the gods or fate have willed should be blind.

While recognizing that this thesis contains valid points, I am inclined to offer a less pessimistic reply to these crucial questions about human nature and destiny. The state of humanity is a serious one, but it can be improved — on certain conditions.

The first condition is that we put our relationship with the biosphere on a new basis. Although we are different from other creatures, we can neither break our bonds with them, nor claim to know precisely how to improve on the myriad links that form those common bonds. Ignoring those facts has led us to commit fatal errors. Thus we have shut ourselves up in our artificial habitats, with only a few chosen species of animals, plants, and herbs — all duly domesticated — for company; but we do not know what the consequences of our isolation may be. In the same arrogant spirit, we are soon going to manipulate, in our laboratories, delicate genetic material in an attempt — probably vain and perhaps dangerous — to improve that part of the living world that interests us. I have already observed that the existing forms of life have emerged thanks to thousands of trials over thousands of centuries, and that any change in the fabric of life can rebound against us.

We must also accept the fact that, from now on, our relationship with our fellow-beings will be subject to much stricter constraints and rules than before. In times past, the law of the jungle could fairly easily be transposed to human societies in order to establish hierarchies of power. Societies were then primitive or very little developed, with scattered populations, and slow and rudimentary means of communication. The situation of modern societies is very different. People are in immediate contact and interact with each other, either physically or through communication systems. Each group, if not each individual, possesses increasing power; their influence can extend very far. To maintain political order and meet moral requirements, therefore, the rule of the strongest must give way to new rules of coexistence, solidarity, and participation.

These simple considerations give very clear signals of the extent to which our modes of thinking and acting must change. They point out that we must learn again almost from the beginning how to live in harmony with the changing realities of these times. *A difficult apprenticeship awaits us*, made still more difficult by the fact that time is inexorably working against us. But that is far from saying that human beings are genetically modelled in such a way that we cannot change, and that consequently we are condemned to bring about our own doom. I maintain that humanity can save itself, and it is up to us to find out how.

Other species do not have these problems. A tiger and a shark know how to be a tiger and a shark. A spider lives like a spider. A swallow is born to be a swallow, pure and simple. Thanks to natural selection, and to the adaptation of their genetic code and their instinct from one generation

solutions for all human problems, one after

ologists were predicting a future in which even
population growth need not pose a problem.
dvocated even modest measures of birth con-
ded as anti-liberal elements; and anyone who
cern over demographic pressures was at once
rophet of doom. It was the time when Her-
the Hudson Institute was introducing his
ept of a 20 x 20 world society — 20 billion
an annual per capita income of $20,000.
goal, it would have been necessary to
s world product one hundred times, but
resist the temptation to believe in the
many scholars and economists echoed
recasts.

were based on *the almost exclusive con-*
e factors. Our generations do possess a
of intellectual and practical resources
ry, ensure the material expansion of
years to come. Our forefathers could
of the immense and growing inheri-
scientific knowledge, technological
ent skill, capital equipment, and
e command. And, in this hopeful
t we have been squandering this
e interpreted as grounds for hope,
far better utilization is possible.
onvinced that the natural resour-
unteous Earth to support human
ing exhausted — could be multi-
uld be developed through tech-

to the next, these creatures ceaselessly improve their apti-
tude to survive by keeping pace with modifications in their
environment. Their present existence proves their success
as species which are the end product of a long evolution. If
at present they are in a very special situation of danger, it is
not because they could not evolve, but because their most
pitiless adversary, their enemy and tyrant — the human
being — is in the process of changing the rules of the game.

We have many things in common with these other creatures. From the point of view of the evolutionary process,
however, we are fundamentally different, for our evolution
has been, is, and must continue to be *an essentially cultural
evolution.* From the dawn of human existence, probably
being unsure of our natural capacity to adapt biologically
in order to survive, we came to rely more and more on our
intellectual and technical resources. Indeed, up against all
kinds of natural obstacles, or in the struggle with other
species, we might easily have been the losers. But, by
shifting the field of competition to our own ground, we
became invincible and were able to rise to supremacy on
Earth. In that way we perfected and equipped ourselves to
pursue a course opposed to that of genetic evolution; and
our evolutionary plan never has been, and could never be,
to alter ourselves biologically of our own accord. It has, on
the contrary, been to alter our environment, and that
makes a continuous cultural evolution imperative.

Each time we have reached a higher stage in our ascent,
endowing ourselves with more advanced tools or more
complex social and political structures, we have had to
learn to live up to the new level we have attained. This is
what we have failed to do at present — hence our crisis.
Having made an extraordinary leap forward in a few
decades, greater than all the progress achieved from the

Middle Ages to modern times, we should accordingly have reorganized our thinking and adopted more appropriate modes of living, that is to say, more compatible with the new and striking heights we had reached so suddenly. However, we have not only failed to understand that such a cultural change is indispensable, and therefore failed to try to bring it about, but we have continued — in our paroxysm of progress — to strive to climb still higher. As a result, we have fallen culturally farther and farther behind a reality that has already outdistanced us.

It is *a paradox that modern men and women are entrapped by their wonderful successes*, which lead on toward others still more brilliant, but which also conceal the quicksands into which we may slip as we move forward. The crucial question therefore becomes whether we are capable of recognizing the vicious circle in which we find ourselves, and of making the supreme effort to escape before we are swallowed up entirely. A great stride forward in cultural quality is vital if we are to survive the new conditions that we ourselves have created.

Although this enterprise will demand all of our intellectual powers of comprehension and imagination, and all of our technical, moral, and spiritual strength, I believe that one cannot affirm *a priori* that success is impossible. On the contrary, I think that *we must give credit to the human being*. If we take the first step — that of realizing the mortal danger in which we stand, and of understanding its causes — other steps will follow.

Before discussing what we will have to do, all of us together, let us try to review the seriousness of the situation of humankind, and the forces impelling us towards further decline.

During these euphoric years, people were not sufficiently aware, among other things, of the depth and breadth of the world's state of disorder. People did not deny the existence of worrisome crises, particularly those affecting the developing countries, nor the disparity between rich and poor; but they would remark that similar situations had arisen throughout the course of human history. And, if it is true that nations have known defeat and decline and have even disappeared, that once glorious empires have collapsed, that entire civilizations have been eclipsed, people emphasized that it is no less true that other peoples, other nations, other civilizations have always superimposed themselves on the losers, allowing the human race to continue its upward progress. People simply refused to believe that in our day any other outcome might be possible; they never stopped to ask themselves whether the entire human system might not one day plunge into disaster. This hypothesis was unthinkable. The destiny of our species could only be constant progress.

A first awakening to reality came in the 'seventies. It was a very different reality from that which people believed in or liked to imagine. The Club of Rome had already sounded an alarm. The publication in 1972 of its first report, *The Limits to Growth,** offered confirmation. The bitter debates that this heretical volume aroused grew even more heated when the oil crisis suddenly arrived in the autumn of 1973. The quadrupling of the world price of crude oil shook to its very foundations the edifice of forecasts and over-optimistic studies of the future, which had

---

* Meadows, Meadows, Randers, and Behrens, *The Limits to Growth*, (New York: Universe Books, 1972). Also available in paperback through New American Library, New York.

been so flimsily constructed over the previous decade.

Almost in parallel with this, the poor grain harvest in a number of countries led the Soviet Union to make massive purchases from the United States, caused a terrible famine in some areas, and forced a disastrous rise in prices everywhere. This demonstrated the vulnerability of world grain markets and the insufficiency of reserve stocks. The prophets of growth at any price were under attack from all sides.

As for The Club of Rome, it did not cease its efforts. Along with the concept of the limits to growth, it had proposed that of *the world problematique*. For there exists in the world a dreadful mixture of problems, whose roots and ramifications we have not managed to grasp, and from which humanity cannot escape.

These are problems of all kinds — uncontrolled population growth, gaps and divisions between peoples, social injustice, hunger and malnutrition, poverty, unemployment, obsession with material growth, inflation, economic crises, energy crises, crisis in democracy, monetary instability, protectionism, illiteracy, anachronistic education, the revolt of youth, alienation, the gigantic size and decay of cities, delinquency, neglect of rural districts, drug use, the arms race, civil violence, abuse of human rights, scorn of the law, nuclear madness, institutional sclerosis, political corruption, bureaucratization, militarization, destruction of natural systems, degradation of the environment, decline in moral standards, loss of faith, a sense of uncertainty, etc. Each of these problems follows its own dynamic of change, and they all interact continuously with one another.

In order to pose the problematique more clearly, my colleague Alexander King has made a diagram of the emerging areas of interdependence (see page 53). At each

Areas of Interdependence

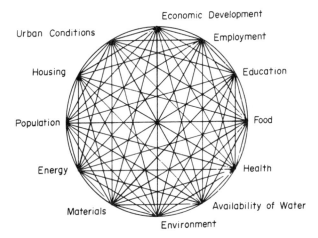

The "world problematique" is illustrated above by the multitude of intersecting lines representing a simplified view of the network of interactive objective factors. However, the human and social factors are excluded.

Source: Alexander King, *The State of the Planet*, Pergamon International Library, Oxford 1980.

nodal point in this network of the problematique, other factors also intersect — social, political, and psychological — creating a highly complex and changing structure. We do not yet possess a sufficiently clear understanding of how all these elements are linked to be able to attack the problematique as a whole. For this reason, each problem is dealt with more or less in isolation, within its own terms, even though these may be only symptoms that we treat to no avail. Consequently, the problematique merely becomes more complicated and the general situation deteriorates still further, giving rise to that endemic state of disorder, insecurity, and crisis which The Club of Rome has called *the predicament of humankind.*

New techniques are, however, in the process of development to analyze the behavior of selected groups of problems and phenomena, so that they need no longer be approached in isolation, but can be dealt with "systemically," seeking solutions that take account of the whole.

The second report to The Club of Rome,* published in 1974, gave an important impetus to these techniques. Others have subsequently been formulated. To mark the tenth anniversary of the publication of *The Limits to Growth,* the state of the art in the field of global modeling was recently the subject of an international symposium convened at the International Institute for Applied Systems Analysis (IIASA). This Institute is a major center of theoretical and practical research on the application of new techniques to the problems of modern societies. A joint East-West initiative based near Vienna, IIASA may play

---

* Mihajlo D. Mesarovic and Eduard Pestel, *Mankind at the Turning Point* (New York: E.P. Dutton & Co., Inc., 1974). Also available in paperback through New American Library, New York.

an unusually important role in the years to come, if a fertile period of collaboration between liberal democracies and socialist countries follows a sterile and dangerous time of tension.

The 'seventies can be considered a period of transition. The oil crisis of 1973, although harsh and salutary, had not struck a hard enough blow to overturn deep-rooted habits and convictions. After all, this proved to be only a mini-crisis. More realistic evaluations of the situation were beginning to be made. But past hopes had not been completely abandoned; public opinion was encouraged to believe in them by the fine words with which those in power are generous when they wish to draw a veil over realities they are incapable of controlling. Besides, people themselves are often prone to all kinds of wishful thinking. They refuse to rack their brains with problems that appear insoluble, or with those that lie in the far-too-distant future and are considered, after all, only of concern to other generations.

But *by the end of the 'seventies the psychological situation had undergone a real change.* The economic crisis was obvious. Oil, the pivot of industrial civilization, was becoming more and more expensive. Gloomy views and forecasts were everywhere. Earlier, people had accused The Club of Rome — unjustly — of being alarmist; now, they were beginning to compete in pessimism.

Furthermore, grave political and military events had arisen to exacerbate an already tense international atmosphere. They followed each other in rapid succession — local wars in Africa and Southeast Asia, more or less directly involving the great powers; the grotesque collapse of the Shah's regime and of his dreams of imposing an artificial form of development in Iran; the Soviet invasion of Afghanistan, following a strategic logic that even the protagonists themselves probably do not understand; Iraq's unexpected and completely inexplicable attack on Iran, involving two potentially rich countries that are in the process of destroying their riches; mounting tensions in the whole of the Middle East and the Sahara; the Polish crisis, with ominous economic implications and potential political overtones; sharpening East-West tensions; the accelerated arms race; the threatened or actual deployment of new nuclear weapons in Europe; the frustrated and uneasy mood of Islam, preparing to use its oil as a weapon. By now, everyone has begun to realize how sick contemporary society is. The risks of direct politico-military confrontation between the superpowers in some part of the world have dealt the final blow to people's spirits. Part of public opinion and many political, financial, industrial, labor, and intellectual circles are seized at present by a confusion and despondency which are the antithesis of the euphoria that prevailed about fifteen years ago.

All these attitudes must be resisted. Just as we had to abandon our naive hopes of yesterday, we must now learn to assess the exceptional gravity of the new world situation in an objective and thoughtful manner. The evidence that our political, juridical, diplomatic, and military systems are on the brink of bankruptcy must not make us lose sight of other dangers. In fact, humanity is also threatened by moral and ecological failure, with incalculable consequences. *Reality must be faced as it is.* On the other hand, we must be careful not to let ourselves be dragged into a spiral of resigned fatalism, nor let ourselves give way to the illusion that a resort to violence holds the answer. The shock of discovering that we are on a collision course with disaster must instead give us the determination to change our course. We have the means. Only by the use of reason, by a sense of our responsibilities, by intelligent application of our resources, by patience and firmness, can we choose a more humane and sensible road for the future, and endure the sacrifices this will involve.

The Club of Rome was formed to this end. It was in April 1968 that a small group of humanists, scientists, economists, educators, and decision makers from the private and public sectors met in the oldest existing academy — the Accademia dei Lincei in Rome — and conceived the idea of founding The Club of Rome. At that time, everything I have just said was not yet very clear. But it was already clear enough that human affairs were being so badly managed that profound changes were becoming urgent. And we were already aware that the very ethical and philosophical foundations of society had to be reconsidered and reformulated, and that the attitudes of individuals and collectivities, from the smallest group to the world community, also had to change to correspond with the real world. The Club of Rome realized that only a cultural development of this kind could propel humankind towards a higher stage of civil progress. To succeed, it was necessary to understand the dynamics of the present and the different futures that might arise from it.

That is the first task to be accomplished now that *we have entered the decisive decade of the 'eighties.*

Ten Factors of Decline

In 1978, on its tenth anniversary, The Club of Rome once again invited important representatives of culture, politics, and practical affairs from about forty countries in the East, West, and South, to gather at the Accademia dei Lincei — this time to examine how the condition of humankind had changed during those ten years. There was consensus that, apart from a few sectoral or regional improvements, difficulties overall had grown in number and kind. And when the enquiry was pursued the following year in a meeting in Berlin, the conclusion was practically unanimous: *the world situation has in fact appreciably deteriorated* and the future prospects for humankind are decidedly somber.

Since then, the evidence suggests that the progressive degradation in the state of the world and the human condition is continuing, and is probably accelerating. Not one major problem has been resolved or attacked effectively, while others are arising ceaselessly, making the whole problematique, in the grip of which we are struggling, much more complex and deadly. Where some progress appears to have been made, it often turns out to be a mirage, or only a temporary improvement.

One example, which concerns so-called peaceful coexistence and is constantly before us, is the strategic arms limitation treaty, SALT II. The two superpowers signed the treaty after years of negotiation, but it is doubtful whether it will ever become effective. Even if it were implemented quickly, the limits it fixes are so high, and technology and military theory — as well as the strategic weapons themselves — are developing at such a rate that the hoped-for benefits would already have evaporated. Another example are the patiently negotiated agreements between Egypt and Israel, with the United States as mediator. They were concluded at Camp David in 1979 as a decisive step toward arrangements that would put an end to the confrontation between Arabs and Israelis. It was an initiative launched with great hopes. Yet it, too, has never been fully implemented. The importance, politico-military and economic as much as cultural, of this part of Asia Minor, where so much history has unfolded for thousands of years, need not be emphasized. But a stable solution to assure peace among its peoples is not yet in sight.

One lesson that these two cases, and others as well, teach us is that time is working against us, and that the great problems of today cannot be dealt with by makeshift methods. It is quite evident that sometimes we no longer know which way to turn; but the reason is that we often refuse to do precisely those things that are essential. We simply seek refuge in what was formerly considered the wise thing to do: we give ourselves a moment for reflection, in the hope of finding the way to a favorable solution. However, these attitudes only foster errors or illusions. Events are racing ahead; we are dealing with highly dynamic phenomena and problems, in which all delay is dangerous. It is more difficult today than it was yesterday to halt the arms race or disentangle the Middle East imbroglio. This applies also to the case of inflation or of drugs, and to the struggle against overpopulation or poverty or social inequality. I shall never tire of saying that we must, without delay, get a grip on our rapidly changing reality; and that we must face up to reality as it is, and not as we would wish it to be for our own comfort.

Ask sociologists, political economists, anthropologists, or philosophers to describe independently of each other *the context of the principal negative factors* which are the basis of the problematique, and which in combination are forcing humanity ever further down the path of decline. The general views they give you will probably be rather different. But their replies will surely identify some crucial points they all have in common.

I consider the following ten factors among the most important:

- *The demographic explosion.* Overpopulation multiplies all existing problems, and at the same time is the cause of immense new ones. To refuse to accept this fact is merely to aggravate the situation.
- *The complete lack of plans and programs* capable of satisfying the essential needs of the vast mass of the world's people and ensuring them a decent existence. Nearly a quarter of the world's inhabitants live in absolute povery and distress; no one knows how many will be in a similar state tomorrow — nor whether they will accept that fate.
- *The devastation and degradation of the biosphere.* The four principal biological systems that support human life —agricultural land, pastures, forests, and fisheries — are being overexploited. Moreover, global ecosystems are threatened by the ravages and pollutions of human systems.
- *The world economic crisis.* Recession, monetary and financial disorders, inflation, unemployment, unrestrained growth, overconsumption, the wasting of resources, and underdevelopment are symptoms of the alarming state of the world economy. The most accessible sources of energy are drying up. Industrial civilization itself is in question.
- *The arms race*, coupled with the progressive militarization of the world. Military budgets are reaching astronomical heights and weapons of destruction possess ever more terrifying capacities. No end is yet in sight.
- *Deep-seated and neglected social evils.* Our society is overcrowded, materialistic, selfish, unjust, and intolerant.

Its bitter fruits are alienation, apathy, crime, drugs, revolt, violence, terrorism, torture, even genocide.

● *Anarchical techno-scientific development.* "Progress" is regarded as an end in itself. It is indifferent to the priority needs of society and to society's absorptive capacity. Its costs and benefits are distributed with the greatest inequity.

● *Old and unadaptive institutions.* These have not kept up with the evolution of life at the national or global levels. Faced with general and increasing pressures, they are being overwhelmed. Political paralysis is spreading.

● *The East-West confrontation and the North-South chasm.* These demonstrate the lack of political and psychological maturity on the part of major human communities and their governments. Under such conditions, the world is ungovernable.

● *Lack of moral and political leadership.* Leaders cannot rise above their ideology, their beliefs, their mandates, or their prerogatives. Not one of them speaks for humanity. The individual remains alone, without guidance, in the dramatic human struggle.

The reader can change the order of these negative factors, add others, or decide to draw up an entirely different list. The result will be the same: humanity is on the decline. And it would be a serious mistake not to realize that, not only is each of these principal factors of our decline alone capable of forcing humankind to its knees, but they reciprocally influence and reinforce each other, creating situations from which there is no escape. It would be even worse to try to break out of the crisis by obstinately persisting with methods and means that have already been tried without success, by merely counting on further material progress, or by relying on false solutions dictated by the logic of force. These paths would only be variants of those that have been followed before. They have brought us to the present situation, and they would only further accelerate our downfall.

Our species has been thrust into crisis at the height of its knowledge and power simply by the incapacity, or refusal, to change its mentality and its behavior, its methods of being and doing, at the very moment when fundamental change and innovation have become indispensable. To remedy this situation and try to perceive in what direction safer paths may lie, let us examine more closely the broad outline of some of the challenges and dangers we must confront.

Human Masses Adrift

The most serious problems of today have grown from yesterday's mistakes, and today's mistakes will multiply tomorrow's problems. *The most distressing of these problems are those which are bound up with the frantic increase in population.* The procreative urge used to be justified by the belief that all children who are born will find their place in the world and will then help their parents when the latter grow old. The large family has a long tradition in custom and folklore, and up to very recent times it has received distinct official and religious encouragement. But human proliferation has become the source of unparalleled misery and suffering.

Examples are countless, but, not wishing to offend any susceptibilities, I shall deal with my own country first. The most incredible bit of bluster on the part of the Fascist regime which flourished in Italy between the two World Wars was the assertion that "in numbers there is strength." In a land with a long history of emigration, and which could not feed all its sons, this position was pure demagogy. The pro-natalist policies that resulted from it, after pushing Fascism into disastrous military adventures in the quest for space for an overflowing population, have, unfortunately, not yet disappeared completely. And they have continued to place a heavy burden on Italy's socioeconomic situation right up to the present day. The demographic factor also had considerable influence on the strategic plans of Imperial Germany and, later, on Hitler's Germany, in the quest for more *Lebensraum*. In the first part of the century, the availability of great numbers of young men in Europe of military age made it easy for the two World Wars to break out — wars that killed tens of millions of people. And history teaches us that there are many other conflicts whose origins lie in excessive demographic pressure.

In spite of its material progress, *humankind still fails to satisfy the needs of all the children it brings into the world*, not to speak of ensuring them a life of minimal well-being and dignity. The fate of one person in four is lifelong hunger, or survival in degrading conditions of ignorance, ill health, and uselessness. The starving people of the Sahel, the Horn of Africa, and about ten other regions, the flood victims of India and Bangladesh, and destitute rural populations of Northeast Brazil, the virtual prisoners in the refugee camps and the people on the margins of society in the shanty-towns of the world, whom we watch on television, are only a few of these doomed inhabitants of Earth. The Dantesque vision of their plight cannot be expressed in numbers. The table on page 64 attempts to do that for

The Deprived People of the World

An estimate for the year 1976. Since then, their numbers have been constantly increasing.

Underfed (below the necessary levels of calories or proteins)	570 million
Adult illiterates	800 million
Those with no access to medical care	1.5 billion
Those with annual income of less than U.S. $90.00	1.3 billion
Those with life expectancy of less than 60 years	1.7 billion
Those living in inadequate housing	1.03 billion
Children receiving no schooling	250 million

From *Basic Human Needs: A Framework for Action,* Center for Integrative Studies, University of Houston, April 1977 (Report to the U.N. Environment Program).

those who live in what are called *conditions of absolute povery* — individuals who can satisfy their basic needs only on the very edge of survival. But the cold statistics lead us to forget that behind each figure is a desperate human being.

As regards *world hunger*, since we cannot get any exact figures and even the criteria of judgment do not agree, we must be content with estimates. At all events, the scene is harrowing. "Our last World Food Survey, held in 1977, is, alas, very revealing: it showed that about 450 to 500 million human beings, mostly women and children, in the developing countries, were seriously undernourished. Several hundred million others were badly fed. The number of people who suffer from hunger and malnutrition is greater than it has ever been, and is increasing all the time."* All commentary is superfluous, except to say that we are all in one way or another responsible for the fact that such situations still exist in our day.

Another grievous and shameful affliction is *that of the refugees*. We do not even know how many there are. Estimates of their number vary, but there are probably about fifteen million. In general, they are the victims of persecution and violence between political factions or various ethnic groups, jammed tightly together in overpopulated areas. Sometimes these forced expatriates are crowded together in conditions of filth and promiscuity in disgraceful refugee camps, without knowing whether they will ever manage to escape and, if so, where they might go. We know the facts of these modern exoduses down to the most anguishing details, but after a few weeks of compassion we

---

* Eduard Saouma, Director General of the FAO. Speech to the European Parliment, Brussels, April 1, 1980.

look the other way. We even prefer not to dwell on the fact that they are merely a symptom of the intolerance that contaminates contemporary society, an intolerance that tomorrow may provoke tragedies of much greater proportions.

Account must also be taken of *the distressing problem of unemployment.* The current definitions of unemployment and underemployment are valid for the developed countries, where one can quantify the number of those out of work with relative accuracy. Owing to varying definitions and statistical difficulties, however, these concepts cannot be applied to the great majority of the Third World. We must abandon indicators that are too precise. In general, the concepts of "occupation" and "activation" are more applicable than that of "employment." Instead of "unemployment," we should refer to the "inactivity" of people, to the impossibility of making use of their capacity for work. For these reasons, the International Labor Organization (ILO) would rather adopt approaches similar to that of absolute poverty mentioned earlier, and to speak of *indigents* who are living below a defined poverty line.

According to ILO estimates, excluding China, such indigents in 1975 numbered 1,103,000.* The majority had no regular employment. To give a statistical sense of the scope of the emerging problem, here are some official data: "The active world population will increase by about 665 million between 1975 and the year 2000. In order to eliminate unemployment and underemployment during that period, it will be necessary to create 125 million productive jobs in the rich countries and 784 million in the poor ones (exclud-

---

* *Medium-Term Plan 1982-87,* (Geneva: International Labor Organization, February-March 1980).

ing China); in other words, for each productive job created in a rich country, there must be six in a poor country."*

These facts should be kept in mind. From now on, to absorb the workers who are currently inactive or will be entering the labor market for the first time, almost 40 million new jobs must be created each year — about double the number achieved in the period 1970-75. As far as I know, in spite of the initiatives of the ILO, concrete preparations to meet this fundamental demand are clearly insufficient if not negligible on the national level, and almost nonexistent on the international level. Consequently, the number of men and women able to work, but who nevertheless cannot find employment of use to themselves and to society, is destined to increase to appalling size. The many consequences of the fact that such a crucial problem is getting out of hand are difficult to imagine.

All these people, marginalized or displaced, owe their unhappy fate *to a society that is morally and socially unjust and economically weakened by excessive demographic pressure* in relation to the resources it possesses or can employ. The classic resource/population equation operates against them. And the gulf into which they are inexorably swallowed can never be eliminated by any national policy or foreign assistance if the terms of this equation are not modified. Like so many others, the problem cannot be understood only in economic, or even in institutional or political terms. It is also, and fundamentally, a cultural problem. We cannot attack it without going to the roots of the evil. Among other things, humanity must learn to

---

* M.J.D. Hopkins, "A Global Preview of Misery and Employment", *International Labor Review,* (Geneva: International Labor Organization, September-October 1980).

reduce its fertility below what is called the "replacement level," and to organize itself to make more rational and harmonious use of all its resources. I refer not only to physical resources — such as water, soil, minerals, climate, tools, and financial investment — but also, above all, to human resources.

The impression that the problems of overpopulation concern the Third World almost exclusively is false. As should be expected in an interdependent world, the consequences of this problem can be seen everywhere in one form or another. Even the developed countries of the OECD,* which used to think they were spared this concern, are now in the line of fire. They are directly affected by a level of unemployment beyond their capacity to reduce, despite the fact that the size of their population is limited in relation to the resources at their disposal. It is estimated that these countries at present have more than 20 million men and women officially out of work, and that that figure will exceed 25 million by 1982. The number of unemployed seems fated to increase still more because of the progressive automation of industry and services. And there are a great number of people out of work who are not included in these statistics.

Associated with this is *the painful phenomenon of migrant workers.* It is sad from the human point of view and sociologically unhealthy. These are generally young

---

* The Organization for Economic Cooperation and Development, consisting of 24 member nations: Australia, Austria, Belgium, Canada, Denmark, Finland, France, Germany, Greece, Iceland, Ireland, Italy, Japan, Luxembourg, The Netherlands, New Zealand, Norway, Portugal, Spain, Sweden, Switzerland, Turkey, United Kingdom, and United States.

people who leave their families and their own cultures to look for work of any kind in richer countries; most often, only hard and low-paid jobs await them, and their economic conditions are inferior to those of indigenous workers. There are already more than 6 million of these migrant workers in Europe. Their number is even greater in the United States, where some of them have a semi-illegal and semi-clandestine status.

The industrial countries will also feel other effects of world demographic pressure. Although their own population levels are relatively low, they will be called upon increasingly to help the Third World, which is being crushed by its growing population. The industrial countries will be forced to adopt flexible policies of assistance and cooperation, quite different from the minimal ones in effect today. They will have to open their frontiers far more generously to the Third World's excess population. And while at the moment they are lands of affluence — rich, wasteful, and relatively carefree — tomorrow they will have to learn a way of life that, if not austere, should at least be sober — an outcome that may, indeed, be to their benefit, too. They will have to abandon their arguments for growth at any price, the deceptive logic of *more* — more production-consumption-employment — for the intelligent logic of *better* — better use of all resources, and particularly of human resources.

Europe, in particular, will find itself facing new problems. Long a great reservoir of men whom it sent to conquer, colonize, and populate other continents, Europe now finds its position reversed. Whereas, in 1800, Europe still accounted for more than 20 percent of the world's population, in the year 2000 it will only have 7 percent. The proportion for each of its major nations — France, West

Germany, England, and Italy — will be only about 0.8 percent of the world total. And everywhere the populations will be relatively old. The old continent will also be old from this viewpoint.

Meanwhile, despite the reduction in size of its active population in relation to its total population, Europe will probably not be able to escape the plague of unemployment. This is a paradoxical situation, because Europe also will certainly have to accommodate increasing numbers of immigrant workers. Its principal problems abroad will be to find new formulae of cooperation and competition with the rest of the world, and above all with its Arab and African friends and neighbors. These countries, young and prolific, in search of capital, technologies, markets, and — more than ever —outlets for their surplus populations, will look primarily to Europe as their closest and most natural partner. They will pose demands that will be difficult to refuse, and difficult to satisfy. Yet, even in this case, the consequences in a way will be beneficial to Europe, too. For, to respond to these demands or simply to survive, Europe will be obliged to develop the ingenuity of its citizens, the strength of its ideas, the appropriateness of its social innovations, the efficiency of its political solutions, and above all its own understanding of the problems of the peoples who need its help. That will demand an extraordinary effort, for which Europeans should unite and begin to prepare themselves now.

Let us return to the world at large. If the situation of the industrial countries is destined to become particularly difficult, the outlook for the overall global situation is truly dramatic. While population problems are growing tremendously, preparations to cope with them are still practically nil — even for so close a deadline as the year 2000. We have not even begun to recognize the unprecedented nature and colossal dimensions of the inescapable task of housing, educating, and feeding the *supplementary population of two billion* that will be added to that already so badly served today. In general, we are mesmerized by the immediate and thus most striking problems, some of which are indeed very serious, such as famine in one particular region or the scarcity of certain nonrenewable resources. But we are not confronting the long-term global problems on which humanity's very fate depends.

Let us take the case of the *physical infrastructure* that will have to be put in place over the next twenty years. This will represent *an entire second world to be constructed from the ground up.* We must design, build, and put in operation thousands of new cities (for instance, of 100,000 inhabitants in size), or large new additions to existing urban centers, and hundreds of thousands, if not millions, of villages (of, say, from 500 to 1,000 inhabitants); and all of these will have to be provided with minimal facilities for a life of modest well-being and dignity. They will need everything: houses, schools, hospitals, public services, factories, workshops, roads, harbors, airports, dams, canals, and silos, as well as opportunities for culture and leisure corresponding to present-day demands.

We shall have neither the time nor the talent to endow these new habitats with anything comparable to the historic and artistic monuments bequeathed to us by our ancestors, which significantly enhance our lives. But, from a functional point of view, this second world will have to be at least equal to the present one, which is not asking very much. Merely to conceive of the challenge makes the senses reel. It is a hundred times more complex than the Marshall Plan, which helped Europe recover after the Second World

War. And the accomplishment would exceed in scope the whole of the construction undertaken by humankind from the Middle Ages up to the present day. These are very complicated calculations, which the reader may wish to check.

In order to comprehend the chaos that will be created by the new waves of population that are certain to break over the Earth very soon, there is no need to examine any other great problems. Those I have sketched here are more than sufficient.

To return to the problem of infrastructure, the fundamental question is: where will this divided human race find the harmony, as well as the creative force, the capital, the materials, and the space for such a tremendous undertaking? To begin with, there would have to be a development plan for the entire planet and its major regions. The conception of this plan alone would require the vision of the great empire-builders coupled with the imagination of the poets, and a total moral commitment to those who are suffering today and those who will follow them tomorrow. But nothing of that kind exists at present.

Under these circumstances, the future can only be dark and stormy. Uncounted masses of human beings will be condemned to be set adrift in a world already overburdened with humans; and they will probably be the cause of the greatest disasters in history.

The Devastation of Nature

The other, more serious medium-term danger is that our generations are weakening or altering the biological capacities of Nature in such a way as to threaten the natural support systems on which the teeming generations of the future must rely.

As I have already pointed out, the spectacular career of the human species has been based on the creativity of our brains and the dexterity of our hands. In the beginning, human beings were scattered in a few places on the globe. Even if we were about to embark on a new and risky adventure, we were, like all other creatures, on the defensive. Yet we succeeded in adding to our territories by making skillful use of our early knowledge and primitive tools, which no other being possessed, and which allowed us to protect ourselves against inclement weather, to gain the upper hand gradually over our enemies or competitors, and to obtain sufficient food — in a word, to assure ourselves adequate margins of survival by making use of Nature for our own benefit. As our position became more and more dominant, this use turned into exploitation, and now that we possess exorbitant power, far beyond our wisdom, it has become overexploitation and devastation.

The first steps of the human species were tentative but, progressively speeding up our pace, we at last embarked on a race for power and built our empire — but too often *on the ashes of Nature*. And we are continuing our inexorable ascent, not knowing whether we may be crossing crucial thresholds or digging our own graves. In this respect, the "noble savage" of the virgin forest, or the wandering shepherd searching for pastures at the dawn of time, however backward they may appear to us, were better able than we are to distinguish between the useful and the harmful. They knew what was taboo, and they did not seek to go beyond their limits. They showed more good sense and more cultural and ecological balance than we do — the barbarians of the age of atomic power and the computer, fiercely proud of our levers and our buttons, our bulldozers, our giant tankers, and our supersonic aircraft.

One of the most important documents of recent times, *The World Conservation Strategy*,* summarizes the situation we have created. I cite it because of its authority:

• The planet's capacity to support people is being irreversibly reduced in both developing and developed countries.

• Hundreds of millions of rural people in developing countries are compelled to destroy the resources necessary to free them from starvation and poverty.

• The energy, financial, and other costs of providing goods and services are growing.

• The resource base of major industries is shrinking.

The consequences are many. One is illustrated by the diagram on page 75. The same publication comments on it thus: "Living resources essential for human survival and sustainable development are increasingly being destroyed or depleted. At the same time human demand for those resources is growing fast. If current rates of land degradation continue, close to one third of the world's arable land (symbolized by the stalk of grain) will be destroyed in the next 20 years. Similarly, by the end of this century (at present rates of clearance), the remaining area of unlogged productive tropical forests will be halved. During this period the world population is expected to increase by

---

* A report prepared under the auspices of the International Union for the Conservation of Nature and Natural Resources (IUCN), United Nations Environment Program (UNEP), and World Wildlife Fund (WWF), Geneva, 1980.

The Living Resources of the Planet Are Decreasing While Population Is Increasing

Arable lands and forests are being reduced at an ever-increasing rate. The genetic diversity of plants and animals is perhaps being reduced even more rapidly, further impoverishing our natural heritage. Humankind, on the contrary, is continuing to increase both in numbers and appetite. Therefore, each individual will inevitably become much poorer in material goods.

Source: *World Conservation Strategy,* International Union for Conservation of Nature and Natural Resources (IUCN), United Nations Environment Program (UNEP), World Wildlife Fund (WWF), Geneva, 1980.

compensate for such a decline. One cannot avoid the conclusion that the problem of human food supply can only
grow worse.

The great *forest areas* are equally doomed or endangered. The natural system demanding the greatest attention is probably that of the tropical rain forests. They are
the vestiges of very ancient biological communities, which
have evolved slowly over tens of millions of years. Under
their shelter, at the present time, live almost half of the
Earth's principal existing animal or plant species. There
also is found the inestimable heritage of the natural genetic
reserves of herbs and plants used in our agriculture — the
first and the last source to which we can turn for biological
renewal.

According to the English naturalist Norman Myers,
these forests are being destroyed at the rate of 50 hectares
per minute, which corresponds to an annual loss of surface
area equivalent to the states of New Hampshire, West
Virginia, and Maryland combined. If we include the forests
that have been converted unsuitably to other commercial
or agricultural uses, the total area lost would be twice as
large, approximating the size the state of California. By
this reckoning, the tropical forests, which still cover some 9
million square kilometers, would only last some 40 years. It
is difficult to imagine our planet stripped of these forests,
deprived of this green belt in its tropical zones. Yet that is
what is happening, and it is not difficult to see that a
mutation on such a large scale will have an enormous
impact on human ecology and health. Yet, for the moment,
nothing seems capable of shaking us out of our cultural or
even our existential insensitivity in the face of this potential
disaster, or of inducing us to control the activities responsible for it.

The most poignant aspect of this whole story is *our relationship with other species*, which have journeyed with us up to now. We need them in great quantitites for our biological existence. They are all important, even those whose practical use we have not yet discovered; and the ecological fabric they form, taken as a whole, is important to us as well, although we are still far from grasping the depth and nature of our dependence. The ravages we inflict upon these other forms of life are pitiless, senseless, and irreparable; these can only be the actions of an insane or savage tyrant.

Believing that we are beyond reproach and therefore can act as we please, we have decimated or annihilated an incalculable number of animal species and plant varieties. We are able to record only what has happened to the major ones, especially the higher mammals that were the most advanced evolutionary forms before the appearance of our own species. To meet our needs, our tastes, or our whims more fully, we capture wonderful creatures and shut them up in cages. We castrate and cross-breed them, inseminate them artificially, manipulate them genetically, overfeed them, and perform vivisection on them. We have specialized and industrialized our agriculture and animal husbandry, going against natural trends that teach us that the more diverse ecosystems are, the stronger and more viable they remain. In all these ways, we ultimately sap the biological vigor and reduce the genetic diversity of the varieties of plants and animals that serve us and that we have domesticated, thus diminishing their resistance to environmental change, to pathogenic agents, and to parasites. And, in so doing, we are with our own hands preparing what tomorrow can become a biological boomerang against ourselves.

From now on, there is a risk that the destruction of other

species will turn into a veritable slaughter. At present, 25,000 plant species and more than a thousand species and sub-species of mammals, reptiles, birds, and fishes are threatened with early extinction. Their evolution had taken whole eras. The same fate awaits huge numbers of small animal species, in particular the invertebrates — mollusks, insects, and corals. As their habitats are destroyed, they will disappear even before science has been able to recognize and classify them. Norman Myers calculates that there are between five and ten million animal and plant species in the world, and that half a million to a million of them will be destroyed by human action by the end of the century. Their future is doomed, while we do not even know what future we are seeking for ourselves, or whether our future may be linked with theirs.

What ignorance of the rules of life, what a waste of potential resources, what contempt for the interests of posterity! What cruelty towards other creatures who also have a right to life, what a lack of culture, what an offense to a true spirit of religion, what a lack of ethical principles and of respect for our very humanity!

Wherever we make an appearance, wildlife — the heart of Nature — is finished. And we are the first to suffer from it. The great American expert Lester R. Brown has demonstrated that the *four principal biological systems* on which we depend, and which I have already mentioned — fisheries, forests, pastures, and agricultural lands — are already overburdened. In spite of increasing investments of capital and technology, world production per capita of certain of their key products reached a peak a few years ago and has now begun to decline. Here are a few examples: the per capita production of wood reached its peak in 1977; that of beef and mutton in 1976 and 1972, respectively; wool, in

1960; grains in 1976; and fish in 1970. To the ancient Chinese proverb that says "Give a fish to a hungry man, and he will eat for one day, but teach him to fish, and he will eat all his life," we must add a note of caution: "on the condition that others don't fish, because there aren't enough fish for all."

It is sad, indeed, to note how many statesmen, economists, and scholars, in spite of everything, reduce all human relationships with Nature to those we have with our immediate environment, concentrating all their attention on the pollution factor. They restrict themselves to tactical considerations, such as the possibility of reducing the most obvious negative effects of human activity on the environment to tolerable limits, so long as that can be done at a reasonable cost. How many times do they remind us of the story of the Thames River, polluted in times past, healthy today! On the strength of this example, they assert, with the pride of those who have solved a problem, that by devoting, for example, 1.5 percent of the national income to the struggle against pollution, it will be possible to bring the latter down to perfectly acceptable levels. This allows them to conclude that we can contrive to have a decent environment without hindering economic growth —and their minds are set to rest.

In order to complete the discussion on this important point, we should have to review a good many other things. It would be necessary to underline the importance for everyone of the potential of the mysterious riches of the Antarctic, among them the famous *krill*, these little shrimp-like creatures that flourish in enormous numbers in the Southern Ocean. For humanity, the Antarctic resources constitute an exceptional biological reserve, protected by a treaty of 1961 which will expire in 1991 — after that, there is a mounting risk of general plunder, for which several nations are already prepared. We should also have to discuss the imminent assault on seabed resources, which will change many things in the oceans, regarded in past times as our perpetual reserve, the common heritage of humanity. We should have to consider the repercussions on the biosphere and climate of the emission of particles and carbon dioxide into the atmosphere; the still little-known effects of the widespread discharge of persistent toxic products and industrial waste; and the reduction of the ozone layer that protects us from the upper atmosphere.

We should have to deal with still other subjects. But the discussion would become too long. And I think that the preceding account of the situation and of the prospects for the human relationship with Nature is sufficient to put us on our guard. The human condition is now a difficult one, and will become precarious. If we do not change our suicidal behavior, we shall soon have to inscribe the human race in the Red Book of the World Wildlife Fund as an endangered species.

The Insane Concept of Security

The most total, most absurd, and most immediate threat to our species is, however, that of *self-destruction by strictly scientific means.* Progress unequalled in other spheres has been achieved to this end. Armaments carefully perfected and with guaranteed results are already in place — nuclear devices, above all. Their use in a wartime situation is planned for the great expanses of the atmosphere and the oceans, which do not present the tedious obstacles of the Earth's surface.

Achievement of such progress has demanded, and still demands, an exceptional effort. The so-called developed countries have engaged a host of scientists who are working day and night, with the support of a formidable military structure and wealthy industries, while the governments and parliaments elected by the people or appointed by the powers that be approve the necessary funds.

Naturally, the superpowers find that this race holds incalculable advantages. But other great nations are also preparing themselves to intervene effectively if there is a nuclear free-for-all, and many countries who are not part of this advanced group are trying hard to catch up. According to experts' predictions, by the end of the century about 40 states will have gained the ability and developed the necessary hardware to join the nucleo-spatial elite.

On the other hand, in addition to the thermonuclear threat, there are other ingenious means — chemical, biological, ecological — which human beings are in the process of testing and developing in order to annihilate their own kind, or at least to paralyze, stupefy, or disable them in hellish ways which our current vocabulary is insufficient to describe.

Thus humanity stockpiles arms — from individual weapons to whole systems of intercontinental ballistic missiles —whose destructive power can only grow. The most powerful bombs of World War II had the destructive capacity of about ten tons of TNT; the atomic bomb dropped on Hiroshima in 1945 was already of the order of 13,000 tons; and at the present time we have at our disposal nuclear warheads with an explosive force equivalent to 25 million tons of TNT. The world's arsenals are full of nuclear weapons, with a total force corresponding to roughly 15 billion tons of TNT. That means that each citizen of the world, children included, is sitting on a charge of more than three tons of high explosive ready to be set off. The diagram at the end of the book gives an idea of the "progress" that humanity has made in this direction in little more than three decades. It is a tale of continuous escalation, and may be the prelude to the end of humanity itself.

In this shocking view of things, we should be fully "satisfied" with the capacity of "overkill" we have attained. But, apparently, this is not the case. Military budgets are increasing all the time, already exceeding 500 billion dollars per year in 1980. It is difficult to visualize what such an astronomical sum represents. It corresponds to one million dollars per minute, or the equivalent every 24 hours of a pile of ten-dollar-bills three times higher than Mount Whitney. This dizzy height of expenditure also allows us to intensify our effort in military research and development, which is already several times greater than that in other areas, including energy.

Half a million scientists — about half the total number in the world, including many Nobel Prize laureates among them — are engaged in the business of "defense." Consequently, we should not be surprised if military technology is taking giant steps forward and if we are, for all I know, on the brink of new breakthroughs that will multiply the "yield" of every dollar invested in armaments. In the box on page 85 there are other indicators of our collective insanity on which to reflect.

Before we ask ourselves how humanity has been able to plunge into such a catastrophic undertaking, I would like to offer for consideration the remarks by some men of high quality and great responsibility. First, those of Robert S. McNamara, the former U.S. Secretary of Defense who has

Some Indicators Of Our Madness

- To keep military expenses at their present levels, everyone during his lifetime will have to sacrifice from three to four years of his income to the arms race.

- The developed countries spend twenty times more on their military programs than on economic aid to the poor countries.

- In two days, the world spends on armaments what it costs the organization of the United Nations and its specialist agencies per year.

- More than 100 million citizens receive their wages directly or indirectly from Ministries of Defense.

- The training of military personnel in the United States costs twice as much each year as the budget for the education of 300 million children of school age in South Asia.

- The price of the Trident Submarine is equal to the cost of maintaining 16 million children in the developing countries in school for a year.

- For the price of one modern tank, 1,000 classrooms for 30,000 children could be built.

- For the price of one fighter plane, 40,000 village pharmacies could be set up.

Adapted from *World Military and Social Expenditures 1980,* by Ruth Leger Sivard, (c) World Priorities, Leesburg, Virginia 22075 and from *North-South: A Programme for Survival,* the Report of the Independent Commission on the Problems of International Development, MIT Press, Cambridge, Massachusetts, 1980.

just retired from the presidency of The World Bank: "No government can escape the responsibility of providing an appropriate and reasonable level of defense for its society. In an imperfect world, that is necessary. But what is just as necessary is to understand that the concept of security encompasses more than simple military force, and that a society can reach a point at which additional military expenditure no longer provides additional security."* The interpretation of this thought is that, beyond a certain level of means of defense — one is tempted to conclude that present levels are implied — *additional* military investments do not increase security, for this would also depend on other, *secondary* factors. Here we have a demonstration of how the judgment, even of the most intelligent among us, is influenced by an obsession with material means. By their extent and their unequalled power, these are reputed to guarantee our society everything, including security and — why not? — salvation. By such an aberration of judgment, we are led to believe in purely technological solutions to social problems, which is one of the reasons for the current global crisis.

The second quotation is from a very interesting and well documented paper, published as part of the research program on problems of war and peace by the French Institute of Polemology: "War, the most violent, the most blinding, the most infinitely variable of social phenomena, remains history's great "Companion" and its strongest matrix. It is the great collective death, the Great Holocaust of men by men, which challenges not only people and families of all

---

* Quoted in Ruth Leger Sivard, *World Military and Social Expenditures 1977* (Leesburg, Virginia: WMSE Publications, 1977).

kinds, but states, societies, and civilizations ... War is at the same time daughter, murderess, and mother of civilizations."*

This statement is accompanied in the paper by reflections on the lessons of history and on the "constance, omnipresence, and inevitability of the terrible phenomenon of war." The latter is supposed to have performed some necessary functions in past societies. But, for contemporary society, the authors recognize that it is indispensable to "channel man's fundamental aggressiveness towards less bloody and less disastrous outlets."

While I could not be more in agreement with the need to direct fundamental human activities as far as possible away from war, I think we are facing here another mental deformation that forces us into a vicious, artificial, and sterile circle. The real question is not to learn how to tame *humanity's alleged innate aggressiveness*. The latter is probably not as dominant as it is said to be, and above all it is not the main human shortcoming. It is too often used as an alibi to conceal more sordid motives. The reasons for the present state of affairs — with some 130 armed conflicts recorded since World War II — must be sought elsewhere.

From the whole of the argument presented up to now, it appears that the situation of the human race today is becoming ever more critical, not because of our supposed aggressive compulsion, but because there is a *chasm between our cultural development and our material power.* In the military sphere, we have the power to unleash apocalyptic forces, but we must only hope that we are never

---

* Gaston Bouthoul, René Carrère, and Jean-Louis Annequin, *Wars and Civilizations* (Paris, 1979).

forced to start using them, because we would not be able to stop. Indeed, while we have acquired the ultimate power to destroy ourselves with weapons of ultramodern technology, we still reason with a pre-technological mentality. We have remained at a tribal and barbaric level in many of our concepts. Face to face with new realities, we find ourselves in such a frightening state of mental confusion that we run the risk, before we know it, of being crushed beneath the weight of our stockpiled weapons, or annihilated in a nuclear holocaust launched by accident, outside of all projected scenarios.

The predicament I have already described, in which we are struggling in quicksand while sinking ever deeper, is therefore of cultural, not biological, origin. We are living under the domination of *the cultural legacies of times long past*. The principle of national sovereignty is one of them; it derives from our ancestral concept of sacred territory to be defended at all costs. I shall return to this point later. The grotesque and paranoid belief that our legitimate aspirations to security can be satisfied by ever more deadly armaments is another such relic. Its ironic and tragic consequence is that humanity, proceeding with insane lucidity to produce ever more powerful engines of destruction, is forced to place all its confidence in the *balance of terror* —which can only be an unstable balance. The entire history of evolution and of the human species is, in fact, studded with collapses in equilibrium followed by the establishment of a new balance. By seeking security in this manner, humanity places itself, paradoxically, in ever greater peril. This is merely one more demonstration of the deranged state of the human mind.

When and how a breakdown in this balance of terror will occur in our age of discontinuities is an open question. It will be a miracle if we manage to avoid it, or keep its most bloody consequences in check. Although I am convinced that, finally, we will not plunge into a nuclear holocaust, I believe that the cultural primitiveness, belligerent behavior, and colossal waste of resources for which our present generations are responsible will impose a heavy and lasting burden on the future of humanity.

The Ambiguity and Ambivalence of Science

To appreciate the influence of techno-scientific enterprise on the future of society, we ought to look more specifically at technology. But we cannot separate consideration of technology from that of science, of which it is an extension — technology being by definition the application of science to practical ends. Science is the humus into which technology sends its roots, and both are currently expanding into vast new zones. Moreover, what today is pure science will tomorrow be applied science, producing a rich harvest of new technologies of various kinds. Let us then consider the whole process under the simple designation of *science*.

Success breeds success, and science is on the crest of the wave. Its accomplishments give it autonomous momentum and stimulate new cycles of research and development and practical applications. Our Marxist friends call this momentum the *scientific and technological revolution*, and assign to it a primary role in the creation of the new society they advocate. But many who are not Marxists also attach great hope to the progress of science as the solution of all human problems, or at least the great majority of them. I have the feeling that, in all this, there is a kind of collective infatuation. Modern society itself has created the myth of science.

Under its noble mantle, how many much less noble designs, however, are smuggled in!

So there are good reasons for exploring the relationship of science with our future. Before embarking on such a delicate argument, I must declare that I stand in awe and admiration of the knowledge that certain scientists possess, and have great respect for many others. And I am the first to recognize that it is thanks to science that humanity has made fantastic progress and can count on making more in the future. Nevertheless, having said that, I believe we must express strong criticisms and serious reservations about certain characteristics and forms of behavior in the world of science. We have seen to what extent it participates in the frenzied arms race — more than any other sector of society, with the exception of the military itself. There are, moreover, other aspects to ponder: above all, *certain ambiguities that characterize the scientific enterprise.*

For example, science, as practiced in our societies, is essentially *at the service of those in power.* In large measure, it is conceived and employed in order to increase their well-being, wealth, power, and prestige. It also serves their whims of overconsumption, whether of material or pseudo-cultural goods. Furthermore, science has become so expensive that it is no longer within the reach of poor societies, but has become the almost exclusive preserve of the industrial nations. According to Alexander King, a foremost expert on this subject, 90 to 95 percent of the world's research and development activities take place there, so that the disparity in this sphere between rich and poor countries is even greater than in income.*

---

* Alexander King, *The State of the Planet* (Oxford, England: Pergamon International Library, 1980).

In other words, the amazing development of modern science is not motivated by the great priority problems of humanity. Rather, it responds to the interests of the developed nations and, more particularly, to the already privileged sectors of their societies, who ultimately derive the greatest benefits from it. The validity of this criticism is confirmed by the confused and inconclusive discussions that have been carried on for a number of years about the transfer of technology to underdeveloped countries, or the endogenous technologies they ought to acquire on their own, or the appropriate or soft technologies that the whole world needs so badly.

Furthermore, one cannot deny the existence of *discrimination in the very heart of science.* Science and science policy are elitist. The panoply of scientific disciplines and their technologies may be vast, but in reality, when it comes to the allocation of funds, only a few are among the elect. Some disciplines are scarcely recognized, and still others remain completely beyond consideration — Cinderellas at the munificent court of science policy. Under the influence of the Anglo-Saxon tendency to limit the concept of science to physics, chemistry, and engineering, it is the so-called hard sciences that carve up the lion's share of investment among themselves.

A corollary observation is that the world of science, which we like to imagine as particularly pure, is on the contrary quite *sensitive to economic considerations.* These take precedence almost everywhere. The life sciences are an example. Their recent great revival is concentrated above all on immediate applications, with an eye to economic profitability. I make this observation not out of moralistic considerations, but because the economic factor works against balanced scientific development. The effect is that the human, social, and moral sciences, which do not promise immediate economic dividends, are relegated to limbo. Yet their importance is growing rapidly. What can be called the "soft underbelly" of society, where the most complicated problems are found, is in need more than anything else of social and political innovation, which the hard sciences, although extolled to the skies, are not in a position to offer us. Only human sciences can.

Another ambiguity derives from our concept of the scientific method. From it, we have developed a propensity for analysis. But we have *neglected the effort to achieve synthesis*, precisely when a holistic approach has become a primary necessity. The more we bury ourselves in analysis, the more we have the impression that we are gaining in knowledge — but often the total picture eludes us. In times past, it was said derisively that information was mistaken for knowledge, and knowledge for wisdom. The truth is that contemporary science offers us an abundance of pieces, or rather fragments, of knowledge without so far providing us that harmony of understanding which is the key to wisdom. And, with all our science and the power that flows from it, it is a little wisdom that we need.

Another criticism concerns the *ambivalence of scientific enterprise*. It can serve to raise the human condition to ever higher peaks, or to degrade it. Even in the past, scientific progress could be directed to good ends or to bad. But today the phenomena deriving from science are far more powerful, and their effects for better or worse many times greater, than ever before.

This dichotomy, inherent in all scientific progress, may nevertheless not be attributed to science itself, which is theoretically without fault, or at least neutral. To find the source of the problem, we must look to society and to its ruling classes, its decision-makers, and its technocrats, to its mercantile or militarist inclinations, to its lack of culture. We must place the blame on error, irresponsibility, selfishness, greed, ignorance, and other human shortcomings in the employment of our gigantic techno-scientific potential.

All the same, scientists are not completely innocent. The weakness they have shown in not reflecting on the improper or immoral uses to which their activities can lend themselves is culpable. No ethical code or social or moral sanction can take the place of the scientists' own sensitivity and sense of responsibility. Furthermore, the question cannot be posed only in the more or less theoretical terms of freedom of research. Modern scientific development is so important that it conditions society and can shake it to its very foundations. What must be considered, therefore, are the relations between the world of science in its entirety and society. And the questions are at the same time social, legal, and practical, going beyond the merits or the rights of researchers or inventors themselves. Now is the moment to remember that scientists form a vanguard, extremely advanced and dynamic, but also very small in number. Even counting assistants and staffs, the scientists of the world number a few million at the most. By contrast, the host of citizens bringing up the rear numbers several billions; and it is this mass that is, or will be, deeply affected *in one way or another* by the actions of the vanguard. The small minority in the lead must therefore learn to judge its responsibilities. It has a duty not to lead the great majority, even involuntarily, into situations that will be still more critical than those now in existence.

To tell the truth, scientists in general have not given too much thought heretofore to the applications of their scientific discoveries and technological breakthroughs, whether for good or ill. This being the case, society has a duty to intervene. It must take every measure to avoid or limit negative applications. As far as possible, this intervention must be preventive. It should take place at the very beginning, through regulations anticipating the scientific activity —for, once the genie has escaped from his bottle, it is impossible to put him back in.

Far be it from me to support the reactionary idea of trying to control the scientific impulse of the inquiring and creative individual; on the contrary, that impulse deserves encouragement and support. But where — by chance, carelessness, inadvertence, or expediency — the scientist's activities can cause serious damage, society must be in a position to impose restraints that have been devised earlier and held in reserve. This rule, by the way, applies to activities in other areas as well, such as the economy, the environment, and political institutions.

This argument is posed with an eye to the future. Indeed, the demand for a vigilant society is growing enormously with newly emerging techno-scientific developments and with new possibilities of their application. *Microelectronics* will relieve humanity of much of the burden of work in the traditional sense, by making possible automation to an extent hitherto undreamed of. This revolution is expected in only a few years' time. Silicon chips smaller than a fingernail, which nevertheless possess a prodigious memory and are capable of infallible performance, will replace the individual in a thousand tasks in manufacture and services. Every human being will enjoy a vast expansion of leisure time. But it will be a long time before either the individual or society will know how to use it. At the same time, *biotechnologies* will intervene. Through the medium of drugs, human engineering, manipulation of genetic material, and asexual reproduction, these technologies will seek to "correct" the constitutional faults of human beings and "endow" them with superior abilities. The task is far more complicated than that which has already been undertaken to perfect the qualities of cattle, poultry, corn, or roses.

In general, these prospects seem tempting, and the risks they pose appear acceptable. People tend to believe that, if these trends create new problems, they also force us to find new solutions, which is seen as the essence of progress. Yet these developments are grounds for deep concern, social in the first instance, philosophical and moral in the second. I confess that I am troubled, even distressed. I suspect that, even more than sorcerers' apprentices, we have become rash fools. On one hand, we are not motivated by the *search for good*, by the desire to use our best abilities to promote it. We are enticed by a spirit of adventure, by the *attraction of the possible*; and we do what we are capable, or what we think we are capable, of doing, without weighing the possible consequences. On the other hand, *we are pursuing fantasies*. We imagine that one fine day we are going to discover a modern "philosopher's stone," which will give us cheap energy, or a miraculous strain of wheat, or a supreme depolluter, even the elixir of youth.

Yielding to the temptations of our new technological prowess, however amazing that may be, we are in danger of *losing our sense of the meaning of life*. As I understand it, that is made up, among other things, of daily application, of the work ethic, of the sweat of our brows and of our calloused hands, of pride in creating and shaping, of being useful and participating; it is made up, too, of the integrity of body and soul, of contact and understanding between

human beings, communion with the natural and the transcendental, of respect for everything that exists. To lose all
that in order to consecrate oneself to science, in the confident hope that it will guarantee us cheap security and
happiness, is rash and foolish. It is a kind of Faustian
bargain that is fundamentally immoral.

On that point I shall end this necessarily brief review of the
dangers threatening humanity — so that I shall not be
carried away by indignation at the fact that our society, so
gifted in many ways, is incapable of establishing a strict code
to govern its own "progress." For no progress, scientific or
otherwise, is worthwhile if it does not carry with it a moral,
social, or political advancement, an improvement in our
customs and behavior, not only in physics, chemistry, or
medicine. In a word, as I never tire of saying, our scientific
progress must be cultural above all.

Two further remarks before I conclude. With regard to
the prospects of microelectronics, a new report to The Club
of Rome is soon to appear. It will critically examine the
relationship between microelectronics and society, and I
hope will succeed in stimulating vigorous and enlightening
debates. Great struggles are also on the horizon in the sphere
of biologic and genetic technology. Important industrial
firms are beginning to invest considerable capital in its
development, convinced that one day they will possess the
key to what they calculate will be a major growth area for
business. This controversy is also fueled by a recent and
astonishing decision of the Supreme Court of the United
States, which recognized that a "new organism" produced
alive in a laboratory can be patented. It may be premature to
deduce from this that everyone will be free to have a private
collection of bacteria or freaks, duly protected by the law.
All the same, scientific circles themselves are uneasy. And

soon there must be a debate on fundamental principles of ethics, and on the legal implications of the creation of artificial life or the substantial transformation of life already in existence.

In conclusion, where is science — *this* science — leading us? If we, as citizens, continue to be its passive subjects, it will carry us off on its powerful wings into the fabulous Ages of Plutonium, Automation, and Genetic Alchemy, which are designed for *Supermen*. But we are still simple human beings, and are almost totally unprepared for life in such ages. And the journey itself, which would extend and exacerbate present trends, is so full of risks that it may plunge us all into disaster. Luckily, other choices are open — if we, as citizens, can understand in time that we must take a direct interest in our own future.

Economic Traps and Delusions

Economics — how many follies have we committed in its name! In order to read its secrets, we have mobilized our greatest talents; to follow its changing whims and moods, we unhesitatingly have devoted the best days of our lives; and in order to obtain its favors, many are the cherished objectives and noble purposes we have sacrificed. But only now are we beginning to perceive the illusions in which this faithless mistress has enfolded us, the traps economics has set for all who have idolized it. Even if our lives were more austere, how much richer they would be if we had devoted ourselves with the same fervor to spirituality, communion with Nature, or human understanding.

We must wake up to the harsh reality that "modern" economics has let us down. Both from the theoretical point of view and in actual performance, *the current practice of economics is out of tune with the fundamental interests of humanity*. It is impossible, in these pages, to give a lucid synthesis of this contrast, complex as it is and controversial. I shall therefore confine myself to a few salient points.

To begin, it is obvious that even the World Bank, such a severe judge on so many occasions and an unequalled source of information, has fallen victim to economic delusions. This great international institution began to publish reports on world development in 1978. The first dealt with the period 1975-85. In it, we read that an annual increase of 4.2 percent in gross national product for the industrial countries and 5.7 percent for the less developed countries would be indispensable if the world economy were to meet then current expectations; and realization of those goals was implicitly regarded as feasible. Now, at that rate, the world economy would double in 15 or 16 years, and in a century would have multiplied no less than 60 times. In spite of the absolute priority given to the economy, such groundless hypotheses should never be advanced even as a dialectic argument.

Clearly, no account was taken in the 1978 report of the limits and constraints that weigh on all human activities. Many people want to continue to deceive their eyes and minds in that way. And it goes without saying that more than one government is taking advantage of that fact to make glowing promises, knowing all the while that its successors will never be able to keep them. There is, moreover, a fundamental hypocrisy inherent in these exercises. We are living in a period that has rightly been called an age of discontinuities. Yet, when we make forecasts for the future, we prefer to ignore this premise in our reasoning. We assume that there will be no changes in the course of events; that the poor people in the world will continue to accept their wretched lot quietly; that unemployment is no more than one numerical variant in the economic equation; that resources and capital will always be available — at prices set by the market — when the economy needs them; and that ecosystems can wait for us to attend to them after the economy has been set on track once again.

It is true that these attitudes are slowly changing. But, unfortunately, real change has come only under the lash of mounting crisis. If we confine ourselves to the World Bank, because of its authority, we can rejoice in the positive evolution its thinking has recently undergone. In its third report on development published in 1980, the World Bank examines global economic prospects in a much more realistic light, and revises the growth estimates cited earlier —although, to my mind, still with too rosy a view of the possible recovery of the world economy. All the same, the report recognizes that, owing to inflation, the oil crisis, and recession in the industrialized countries, the greater part of the Third World will face very hard prospects during the 'eighties, and that absolute poverty will spread throughout Asia and Africa.

The remedies proposed nevertheless remain the traditional ones, even though they have not succeeded in avoiding the present crisis. They are essentially made up of technical measures which are patently inadequate to confront problems that are rooted in the diseased body of society itself. And, when structural reforms are considered, the report seems to imply that all that is needed is to change the roles of the actors without modifying the rules of the game and the framework within which it is played. Finally, pious hopes are expressed — that the Third World may make better use of its resources; that the industrial nations may renew their growth, increase their foreign aid, and liberalize trade; that the oil-producing countries may recycle their capital more wisely. It is a sad illusion to hope that the world economy will be restored to health through a mixture of such remedies. If we come to realize this in a few years' time, it will be too late.

It is also true that some economists are beginning to make room for the necessity of human development as one of the elements that must underpin economic progress. They refer almost exclusively, however, to the Third World as if the problem of raising the quality of the actors — so that, instead of simply being bit players in the cast, they might assume leading roles — were peculiar to that part of the world! Moreover, their sights seem to be set on the development of human robots — machines for producing and consuming —so that greater efficiency can be achieved and the economy improved. We shall see later how universal and wide-ranging human development must, on the contrary, be. But even now it can be stated that it is terribly petty to regard the human being as solely a function of material growth. Such reasoning is full of old conceptual errors, for a healthy economy is not necessarily an affluent economy, and still less an economy addicted to meeting artificial needs.

One must not misunderstand these criticisms. It goes without saying that *economic activity is a fundamental human activity — but it is being poorly managed.* It is fundamental to the well-being of the individual, to the blossoming of the personality, to civil progress, and to the cultural enrichment of society. But, if ill conceived or badly managed, it also can be the principal source of social injustice, of the enslavement of the individual to the machine, or his subjugation to others. It is economic activity that has the greatest impact on the environment, and that, in one way or another, shapes our relationship with Nature — and demands the best and most productive years of peoples' lives. In the existence of Third World peasants, who make up more than half the world's population, hours of work certainly far outnumber those devoted to physiological needs and all other activities.

This basic fact is therefore not subject to debate. What we must examine critically, beyond this point, is how we conceive and conduct our economic enterprise. Is it not absurd that such a crucial activity should be governed by principles and procedures of a far distant past, with an obsession for growth — of whatever kind — and sectoral ways of thinking, at the mercy of special interests? And that this bad management should be accompanied by a remorseless waste of natural and human resources? Is it not equally incredible that, at the same time, industrial societies do not know how to make wise use of their technical resources? And that, to maintain themselves, they have created a staggering number of fictitious financial resources — close to a trillion dollars, it would seem — which different countries are borrowing from each other, and from the future, and which one day may cause international financial markets to collapse like a house of cards? Or that, to revitalize their economies, the principal nations should depend on military expenditures, without which they would be in even worse shape than they are today?

Such a state of affairs can be explained only by the fact that we have not yet grasped the overwhelming dimensions and revolutionary character of the phenomena that we shall be called upon to face in the coming years. Unfortunately, the results speak clearly for themselves. The world is in the coils of a deep, complex economic crisis, from which no way out can be seen. To understand this better, we need only examine a little more closely that unambiguous symptom, the *growing economic disparity between the industrial countries and the Third World.*

We have become so used to the fact that a serious, ever-widening gap exists between the two that we treat the question as routine, a constant feature of contemporary society. We do not realize that this gap is in the process of being transformed into an abyss that imperils the entire human system. Yet the facts are clear enough. The graph on page 103 depicts with brutal frankness the unsustainable situation that will develop by the end of this decade. It is provided by the World Bank, along with the following figures.* From 1975 to 1999, the average personal income (expressed in 1975 dollars) in the industrial countries, which will then contain 13.6 percent of the world's population, will rise from $5,865 to $9,999 per year. For the Third World, a reasonably favorable forecast for the period 1980-1990 indicates that personal income in the less poor countries, then comprising 25.2 percent of the world's population, will rise (in 1977 dollars) from $1,275 to $1,719, and in the poorest countries, which will account for 31.6 percent of the world's population, from $168 to $206. Thus, according to these forecasts, by 1990 the inhabitants of the wealthy countries will have at their disposal *an annual income of almost 50 times greater* than that of the inhabitants of the poorest countries. And if one were to take into account the devaluation of the dollar between 1975 and 1977, this gap would be even greater. Is it possible to believe that so many people will be able to live in peace in

---

* These are extracted from World Bank reports on development for 1979 and 1980.

Trends in Gross National Product Per Capita, By Country Group, 1960-90

Dramatic evidence of the explosive situation in which the world finds itself is provided by the divergence of these curves of economic development. Less than one-seventh of the world population is making economic headway. The great majority is not keeping pace.

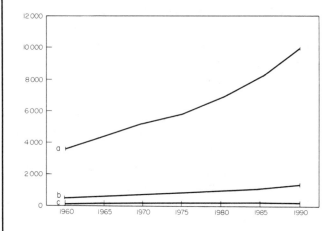

a = industrialized countries
b = developing countries with medium revenue
c = developing countries with a low revenue
(Socialist countries are not included.)

World Development Report, 1979, The World Bank, Washington, D.C., August 1979.

such a small world on opposite sides of such a deep gulf?

The reality, however, is even worse than these averages lead us to believe. For they do not take account of the economic disparities existing within the areas under consideration, which are sometimes even greater than the disparities between nations. Our shrunken, overpopulated, and overarmed world is riddled and torn by economic disparities, which are not only rationally unjustified and morally unacceptable, but now also politically intolerable. To continue to pursue a policy of business as usual means that an already very difficult situation will be transformed into an explosive one.

Here, a few more words must be said about *the dramatic problem of employment.* The very logic of the economic enterprise demands that we conserve expensive human labor, and instead rely on cheaper labor performed by machines or microcircuits. These replacements for human beings are becoming ever more efficient and more productive. They have been the means of freeing the worker from heavy, unpleasant, or unhealthy tasks, and of expanding productivity. Reality also has another face, however, for these machines at the same time can subject the worker to the control of mechanical or electronic devices, and even eliminate the need for his labor altogether. The individual can be pushed out of a job, marginalized, by a tiny, anonymous "chip." It is a delusion to believe that automation will ultimately create more jobs than it eliminates. If society is incapable of modifying its concepts of economics and work, automation carried to the extreme will, on the contrary, become the cause of structural unemployment. The growing discrepancy between the requirements of the economy and those of the common good would then become manifest, and we would face a new range of virtually insoluble psychological, social, and political problems.

Indeed, the equations that we must solve have changed or are in the process of change, but our vision of the economy has not been able to keep pace. As I have already stated, the deepening crisis leads us to seek escape through inadequate measures, palliatives, policies unsuited to the emerging conditions. Particularly negative among these are policies designed to support global demand for goods and services at a time when we know that the natural resource base is being consumed, and that the provision of those goods and services will demand the application of technologies that are increasingly costly and more consumptive of energy. We are still *captives of the myth that exponential economic growth can go on forever.* Our obstinacy in pursuing this impossible goal will cost us dearly. The consequences are inescapable. They lead inevitably to scarcity of certain elements or products in the market and continuously rising prices, in short to a situation of chronic inflation and monetary chaos that encourages speculation at the expense of serious enterprise.

In this way, *inflation* and *recession* are added to the problems of the *disparity between rich and poor* and *the devaluation of human labor.* These four horsemen of the economic apocalypse are lying in wait for humanity, feeding on its disorders and imbalances, profiting from its mistakes. We have reached a point at which *our basic economic concepts must be thoroughly reexamined —* from wealth to product and from welfare to value. They are out of step with the realities of our times.

My colleague Orio Giarini attempted to contribute to this essential renewal of our economic thought, and succeeded in doing so in a recent report to The Club of Rome, published under the title *A Dialogue on Wealth and Wel-*

fare.* This very interesting and well-documented book, along with the rising tide of other new economic thinking, is destined to open a debate that I am sure will be particularly fruitful.

I only have time to mention in passing some of the main arguments Giarini develops. He begins by attributing an economic dimension to the natural environment: economy and ecology are inseparable, and each is part of the same whole. Wealth and welfare cannot exist in a world that is ecologically unhealthy. Strategies aimed at increasing wealth must be centered on the reality of that primary common inheritance that is the Earth. And the strategy of the production of wealth cannot be separated from that of the conservation and sharing of this inheritance. Real value is not represented by the cost of production, but is dependent on the utilization over time of products and services, which thus shifts the emphasis to their usefulness and durability. Activities that produce wealth but destroy part of our natural heritage may, in fact, create a negative value, or "deducted value." There can be no economic progress without prior or parallel human development.

In conclusion, a new and revolutionary vision is perhaps even more vital in the world of economics than in that of science. Without it, another great bastion of the empire that modern men and women have created with so much ingenuity and hope may collapse — dragging down with it a great part of the human system.

---

* Orio Giarini, *A Dialogue on Wealth and Welfare* (New York: Pergamon Press, 1980).

Humanity Crucified

Our generations have transformed the environment and our way of life beyond all imagination. But *our social and political organization has not undergone a comparable evolution.* To a large extent, it is outdated and inadequate, and represents one of the principal factors in the decline of human fortunes.

In this century, humanity has tried in vain several times to create a new world order. The Marxist revolutions are an example of a grand design that remains incomplete, or at least far from achieving its expected goals. World War I was of no more use in this regard; the attempt 60 years ago to bring order to the world through the League of Nations met with failure. After the Great Depression of 1929, the unfortunate growth of extreme nationalism led to the division of peoples, and finally to the bloodiest of all wars, World War II.

The transformation of power structures and the process of decolonization that followed this conflict stressed the need for profound changes in international organization. The creation of the United Nations system represented an important innovation, but today, after little more than 30 years, it is no longer sufficient. The present world crisis is in part a crisis of this system, as well as of a series of concepts, from American-Soviet bipolarity to the division of the planet into spheres of influence, which formerly seemed to give a certain stability to world society. Yet the world is not succeeding in becoming multipolar, as many had wished. The so-called "non-aligned" countries — remaining neutral of the great powers — proposed themselves as a new element, a kind of third force. But their group is too heterogeneous and split by internal dissensions to form the nucleus of a new world structure.

The structural faults of contemporary society, moreover, begin at its very foundations, which are old and inadequate. The international order that we have been able to build on such a base is really only a conglomerate of national sovereign states bound to each other by formal rules which, whenever it appears expedient, are not respected. Each of these states —whether of a socialist or liberal inspiration, and with an authoritarian, democratic, or even theocratic government —insists intransigently on its sovereign rights. Yet *the principle of national sovereignty is one of the major obstacles to the collective salvation of humanity.* A few years ago, the great English historian Arnold J. Toynbee declared that sovereignty "has become mankind's major religion, a religion whose god is a Moloch to whom parents are willing to make human sacrifices of their sons and of themselves and of all their fellow human beings too, if a conventional war should escalate into a nuclear one."

The nation-state, sovereign over its territory, deserves special mention. Developed in Europe as a means of escape from feudalism, the nation-state was established by the Treaty of Westphalia, which in 1648 brought an end to the Thirty Years' War. Europe, covered with forests at that time, had practically no means of communication; the few people who travelled went on foot, except for a small privileged elite who could pay for a horse or a very uncomfortable carriage; and the few people who could read did so by daylight or by the dim light of oil lamps. Everything has changed since then — except the cult of territorial sovereignty. The astonishing fact is that, in this age of space exploration and atomic energy, not only has this relic of a past epoch remained the functional unit of world political organization, but its application and its harmful effects are expanding, without provoking any great reaction.

Before World War II, there were about 60 sovereign states, some of which possessed very extensive colonial territories. At present, there are about a hundred more; of these, 155 are members of the United Nations. Their frontiers have constantly shifted backwards and forwards over the course of centuries. Sometimes they were fixed by the whims of potentates, by dynastic marriages, or backroom deals; sometimes they sprang from the fantasies of cartographers charged with tracing the spheres of influence of the colonial powers. Yet each country — large or small, old or new, representing a logical national unit or having only modest historic, ethnic, or geographic justification for its existence — is jealous of its sovereign prerogatives and declares its frontiers to be sacrosanct and untouchable.

These solemn declarations are often merely a camouflage —sometimes pathetic, sometimes hypocritical — for an embarrassing or sordid reality that the powers that be prefer to hide from the general public and manipulate behind the scenes. Without even mentioning the concept of "limited sovereignty" recently affirmed among the socialist countries, one can state that — in relations with the superpowers, with other strong nations, or even with large multinational corporations — the sovereignty of small states in practice has only a nominal value. Furthermore, one would not be far from the truth to say that very few are the states, which, however liberal in other matters, are ready to accord the same rights of identity and independence that they claim for themselves to the ethnic and cultural minorities placed within their frontiers by the accidents of history.

The crimes perpetrated under the cover of the rights of sovereignty are among the worst. Oppression spreads and conflicts smoulder or erupt within nations, and minorities are persecuted, without the international community being able or willing to intervene — the way being barred by the taboo of sovereignty. The time elapsed between the American intervention in Vietnam and the Soviet occupation of Afghanistan was short. Yet, during this brief period, a striking number of countries have been torn apart by internal struggles, at times medieval in their cruelty, or have plunged into conflict to redress alleged wrongs or defend hypothetical rights. Laos, Cambodia, Malaysia, Indonesia, India, Pakistan, Bangladesh, Iran, Iraq, Timor, Ethiopia, Somalia, Sudan, Uganda, Zimbabwe-Rhodesia, Mozambique, Angola, Chad, Nigeria, Western Sahara, Lebanon, Cyprus, Northern Ireland, Chile, Argentina, Bolivia, Nicaragua, and El Salvador are among them. The list will certainly grow longer in the years to come.

The cult of sovereignty has become so much a part of our way of thinking that we can no longer perceive its incongruities, nor the real interests it serves and its long-term costs. One must stand back and look at the world as a whole to be able to see the kaleidoscope of states into which continents are carved, with their claims extending into the oceans as well. It is then even more staggering to contemplate what the beneficiaries of sovereignty have managed to invent in order to justify and perpetuate this dismemberment of the human family.

The excessive growth of military forces, extorting six percent of the product of human labor every year, is not the only support on which this senseless partitioning of the world can rely. In addition, there is a proliferating diplomatic network and a burgeoning array of information or propaganda services. Their usefulness is certainly in question at a time when radio, television, and the press put the news within everybody's grasp; when the telephone, telegraph, telex, and airlines span the world; when scores of satellites are constantly on station over the Earth; and when journalists disclose everything that is even remotely of interest. These superstructures can titillate the taste of a public that loves military display, fanfares, parades, regalia, secret funds, and cloak-and-dagger novels to such a degree that they forget how superfluous and costly all this is. Their principal *raison d'être*, however, ought to be clear — it is *above all to serve the interests of the ruling classes.*

If territorial sovereignty remains the keystone of world order, and if its trappings are accorded unparalleled privilege, it is because they both are in fact as indispensable to those in power as the air they breathe. The sovereign state is their fiefdom. Its pomp, its rhetoric, and its egocentrism suit them no less than its structures and superstructures. The enforcement of sovereign rights protects their position, sometimes in the name of homeland and tradition, sometimes in the name of homeland and revolution, or in the name of other symbols. The state offers those in power endless means of influencing citizens both psychologically and politically, of brainwashing them or stirring up their nationalism or chauvinism. That is why officialdom in every country, from the most conservative to the most progressive, is unanimously opposed to those who dare affirm the subversive truth that the orthodoxy of the sovereign state, besides being dangerous, is untenable and perfectly ridiculous in the modern world.

Humankind has paid an incalculable price for having dogmatically retained this Kafkaesque political organization. The price is exacted not only in all manner of wars and conflicts — including the two great world conflagrations. It is almost as heavy in peacetime. Added to the direct costs are those of subsidies to industries established on non-competitive national bases, of protectionism, of economic and intellectual autarky, of education tainted with nationalism and blind to world affairs. No-holds-barred competition forces selfish states to rely on deceit, to falsify history, to manipulate the press, to stuff people's heads with tales, and to invoke "reasons of state," which almost always conceal motives that cannot be exposed. All this poisons the international atmosphere. The citizens of the world are forced to live in a climate of hypocrisy, half-truths, baseness, and expediency which sap their character and destroy their sense of reality.

At a time when fearful and decisive challenges loom on the horizon, humankind can no longer tolerate being kept in such an ethical and political twilight zone. Some of the consequences of this condition of weakness have begun to be manifest within nations that are incapable of coping with their own problems. They are seized by *the subtle and insidious evil of political paralysis*. This situation can be observed in different degrees and in different forms in a number of countries. One might mention Poland, Turkey, and Iran, for example. The same evil is threatening Italy and other European nations as well as many of the less developed countries, and it seems to be spreading epidemically. This political paralysis has passed from states into the international sphere. The system of nation-states, in effect, is acting as a kind of catch basin for all the faults, weaknesses, and contradictions of its members.

That is why the important Madrid Conference, inaugurated with such difficulty in November 1980, is merely marking time. It had been convened in order to continue and complete the work of earlier conferences in Helsinki and Belgrade on European security and cooperation. But, in all probability, it will achieve at best only further accords that are almost completely devoid of content or effectiveness.

Another disappointing example of the inefficiency of the present international system, unable to reach agreement on either essential principles or questions of detail, is provided by the "global negotiations" initiated at the United Nations. They should have launched a strategy for the "Third Development Decade." As everyone knows, the first two decades ended in frustration. That of the 'eighties risks being doomed from the outset to the same fate. After interminable preliminary consultations and many months of intensive preparation, at the time of this writing not even the rules of procedure and the agenda of negotiations have been conclusively defined.

It is time to recognize that, in its present form, *the world is both structurally and politically ungovernable.* In the current state of affairs, there is absolutely no possibility of instituting a "New International Economic Order," and even less the "more equitable and sustainable" order of which we dream. Only the "great disorder under the heavens," denounced by Chairman Mao, can continue to reign.

The essential problem to resolve is that of incompatibility between the existence of the inward-looking, sovereign nation-state and the well-ordered management of human affairs on a global scale, which has become a fundamental imperative of our times. On the other hand, we must be realistic enough to recognize that it would serve no purpose to attack the nation-state or the principles of sovereignty which are its prerogative, without having anything to offer in their stead. New models of global political organization are being studied in several places, but their elaboration will require a great deal more time. So we must proceed in stages.

I think that, at present, the most urgent and essential task is to eliminate the principal obstacles to governability in the world system, without substantial structural change, in order to gain greater freedom of maneuver and prepare in an orderly way for later steps.

Two of the causes and principal consequences of global political disorder are the permanent state of tension between East and West and the fundamental imbalance between North and South. Humankind is crucified along these two axes. It would be a great step forward simply to recognize that, if these situations persist, there will be no means of governing the world and the way will be open to catastrophe.

As we know, the protagonists of *tensions between East and West* are primarily the Soviet Union and the Socialist countries of Europe, linked by the Warsaw Pact, on one side, and the nations of the Atlantic Alliance, whose leader to a large extent is the United States, on the other. For the moment, we can leave out of the picture the great nations of the Far East — China and Japan — since their inclusion would not change the logic of the discussion.

We also must recognize that East-West tensions are based on rivalries between sovereign states, or between the classes that represent them, and not on disputes between peoples. The latter, even at the risk of considerable sacrifice, would very much like to see the tensions and their attendant dangers disappear; and they are far from understanding all the reasons advanced by their governments to defend their own positions and to condemn the intrigues and maneuvers of their adversaries. The main conclusion to be drawn, however, is that, so long as the East-West antagonism continues — that is to say, so long as one of the main preoccupations of the superpowers and their allies or clients remains that of obstructing what the other side is doing — no real progress in human society is possible. If there were ever any doubts on this point, the events of the years 1980-81 were sufficient to eliminate them.

As far as North-South relations are concerned, we must not delude ourselves. The gap separating the rich and poor of the Earth has not ceased widening since we started to investigate it. And, as we have seen, it will continue to grow wider, deeper, and dramatically worse — despite all the resolutions passed by the United Nations, despite all the efforts of the less-developed countries themselves, and despite all foreign aid policies that may be adopted by some developed countries. For this gap is, in effect, a structural, seismic fault, arising from *a fundamental asymmetry between North and South*, which in turn hinders all real progress in the world.

This asymmetry is shown in graphic form on page 116. In the North, we see giants; in the South, an array of nations with far less economic, technological, and political power. The four techno-economic colossi in the North of the planet are obeying the logic of giants who have attained the dimensions and power necessary to guarantee their own substantial self-development. These are, of course, North America (the U.S.A. and Canada), Western Europe,* the U.S.S.R. with its allies**, and Japan. They are very different from one another. All the same, on certain fundamental questions they tend to develop the same interests and to behave in the same way. To this roster we can add China,

---

* Essentially, the expanded European Community.

** The Council of Economic Mutual Assistance (CEMA), better known as COMECON, composed of Bulgaria, Czechoslovakia, Democratic Republic of Germany, Hungary, Poland, Romania, and the Soviet Union.

The Planet Out Of Balance

In the North: a few techno-economic giants.
In the South: more than a hundred nations which are techno-economically small or medium sized.

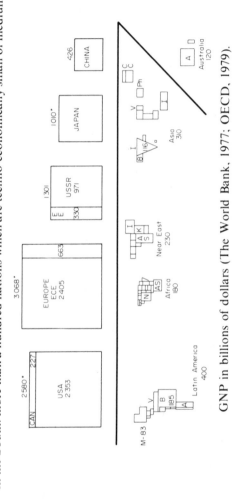

GNP in billions of dollars (The World Bank, 1977; OECD, 1979).

Source: Adapted from a study by Maurice Guernier for The Club of Rome, December 1980.

which is preparing to become the fifth among the giants —
and perhaps, in time, the first.

In the South, by contrast, there is a multitude of individual countries — about 120. Although some of them possess a nearly numberless population, they all have only limited technological capacity and their economic dimensions range from average to small, even minuscule. From the economic point of view, Brazil and India are the largest. Their gross national products are nevertheless not much greater than that of Spain, and markedly less than that of Italy, which are merely two provinces of Europe. Without making a fetish of the GNP, we can occasionally use it for reference, and in this case it gives us an idea of the vast structural imbalances between the developed countries and the Third World.

In the next few years, the latter will also have to face up to terrifying difficulties. My colleague Maurice Guernier has given us a lucid exposition of this prospect in his recent report to The Club of Rome.* He takes account of other specific factors beyond the demographic explosion, such as the generally tropical condition of the Third World, which makes agricultural development difficult; the lack of adequately trained professional and managerial elites; social structures inappropriate to the demands of technological development; economic distortions brought about by international aid even when foresighted; and free international trade which ends up by imposing the law of the most powerful. The developing countries must struggle with all these difficulties simultaneously. And no matter what, it is

---

* Maurice Guernier, *Tiers-Monde: Trois Quarts du Monde* (Paris, France: Dunod, 1980).

a struggle that, with rare exceptions, they are fated to lose.

To have any chance of success, the countries of Africa, Latin America, and Asia ought to unite not only at the diplomatic conference table and in voting at the United Nations, but also in practical action. At present, their greatest enemy is the emotional and myopic nationalism they have inherited from Europe which, applied in their own lands, has often become micro-nationalism. This nationalistic spirit helped the Third World in the anti-colonial liberation movement and in the creation of their first independent political structures. But it has now become a negative factor of great weight, at least to the extent that it hinders the formation of larger political and operational coalitions capable of attaining goals that are beyond the powers of smaller and weaker individual states. It prevents their achieving a relatively autonomous socio-economic development and a position of equality in the dialogue with the North.

I shall return to these points later. The idea I want to convey, in concluding this chapter, is a simple one. We have reached the dawn of a very difficult and decisive period, in which humanity must make supreme efforts to survive. Yet we are so far incapable of doing so because we are paralyzed by outmoded political conceptions and obsolete institutions, and crucified by the incompatibilities and lack of communication between East and West and between North and South. In such conditions, political and military confrontations are inevitable. It is up to our generation to find a way out of this impasse before it is too late, and to prepare the way for the billions of inhabitants on the planet to organize themselves into societies that at last will be governable and peaceful.

The Roots of Our Downfall

The factors of decline that we have reviewed are unfortunately so considerable that we cannot conceal from ourselves the fact that humankind is on a slippery slope to disaster. If, on one hand, it is impossible to establish how, where, and when the real disasters will begin, and how they will spread, it is clear, on the other, that to avoid them it will not be sufficient to correct just a few faults here and there.

It is absolutely essential for human society to change course. I shall discuss this further in succeeding chapters. But, to understand how it can be done, *we must deepen our analysis of the human factor*, return to the individual human being, who is more than ever the protagonist of this adventure. We have seen that we have overpopulated the Earth, and that this avalanche of population growth has been, and will increasingly be, the great multiplier of all other negative factors. Yet, until recently, the ruling circles of the world preferred to ignore the problem and the terrible consequences of growing demographic congestion. The declarations by the majority of the participants in the United Nations World Population Conference, held in Bucharest in 1974, testify to this fact. It is only in recent years that we have begun to speak openly about population growth, but we still do so in a hesitant and reluctant manner. Moreover, every time governments and experts get down to population problems, they devote their efforts almost exclusively to *population as a quantitative issue*.

Individuals are considered primarily as biological organisms, economic entities or, more specifically, consumers. Attention is concentrated on their material demands, or on their potential for political or electoral revolt, their tempta-

tion to resort to the barricades if those demands go unsatis-
fied. Other basic cultural and spiritual human needs, as
well as expectations and aspirations, which have no power
to cause upheavals and disorders, seem to be relegated to a
secondary level. More generally, the human individual is
seen only as the cause of problems, not as the potential
source of their solution. In fact, *the qualitative aspect of the
population* enters the picture almost exclusively when education and professional training are discussed — which, by
the way, is frequently done with a very limited perspective.

Contemporary society is, in fact, so focused on material
objectives and problems that its principal aim seems to be
to teach people how to do certain specified things. Education and training are geared to this purpose. Society
scarcely devotes any time to the necessity for people to
learn how to live in a responsible manner, in harmony with
today's realities, or to the resulting need to develop the
human personality and untapped potential in order to
respond to this primary requirement. In other words, problems and policies with regard to population are envisaged
without taking account of the key factor of *the quality of
the citizenry*, their capacity to face up to the unusual challenges and to seize the equally unusual opportunities of our
times.

And yet, it is precisely the quality of the protagonists that
counts in the human venture, whether we are dealing with a
village, a nation, a region, or the world. It was the human
quality that counted in the grandeur of Greece and the
glory of Rome, and in their decadence as well; in the
wonderful scientific and civil developments of Islam, as in
its decline; in Spain's conquest of America; in the rise and
fall of the British Empire. Again, it is the quality of the
Japanese people that makes their nation what it is, and that

of the inhabitants of other countries that has led to their internal crises. And it is certainly the quality of its citizens that can make a city pleasant and prosperous or filthy and decadent; and the quality of the members of a family that can bring it happiness or ruin. And, finally, it will be the qualities of the inhabitants of this planet that will determine whether or not they will be able to live here in peace, without killing each other, when their numbers have reached five or six billion.

It is obvious that the qualities that were necessary in the past to master oneself and triumph over others, to found a civilization, or to solve problems are very different from those needed now. And, even in our day, in the different cultural, social, and political milieux of the peoples who make up the mosaic of the world, the requisite human quality should have a common denominator but can consist of many different components from one situation to another.

To be "human" in the fullest sense has always demanded special qualifications. In the beginning, it was but *a kind of craft*, requiring certain intuitions and capabilities that the individual had to develop as he progressed towards more highly evolved forms of society. Next, it became *a more and more complicated job* demanding more refined qualities and expertise, which people managed somehow or other to attain on their own in order to cope with the problems and avail themselves of the opportunities that were emerging in different epochs. At present, to be human has become *a highly sophisticated profession*, which cannot be carried out without training and ability of an even higher order. This level of human development has not yet been reached either by us, whatever our position may be, or in general by our contemporaries. Human beings are still mediocre in relation to the qualifications that we ought to possess to fulfill our functions in this new age. This is why we find ourselves bogged down in virtually insoluble problems.

To tell the truth, modern men and women have devoted a great part of their talents to expanding and perfecting certain qualities and capabilities, while neglecting others. As a result, *two cultures exist within us, but we are possessed by a single one.* We are thus out of balance, in a state of confusion; we act inconsistently, like schizophrenics. There is a real gulf between the power and impressive breadth of our scientific knowledge, our technical skills and devices, our machines and our super-modern equipment, our systems of communication, production, and destruction, on one hand; and our outdated concepts of security, of sovereignty, of growth, and even of the future, our outmoded institutions, our ancestral totems and taboos, and our ineffectual rites and ceremonies for invoking peace, justice, development, or democracy, on the other.

We have stolen from Nature the secret of nuclear fission, but we use it mainly to mass-produce bombs. We know how to combat many diseases, and thus have managed to double the average life expectancy, but we have not learned how consequently to regulate our fertility. We produce all kinds of goods on an unprecedented scale, creating bottlenecks in certain regions that are choking with plenty, while elsewhere the Biblical scourges of poverty and famine continue to rage. We have set off to conquer the cosmos, after conquering Earth, but we still do not know how to manage our own planet.

These imbalances and contradictions are anchored very deeply within ourselves. The roots of our downfall are

The Distortion of Homo Sapiens

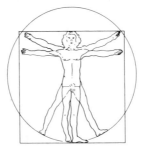

Harmonious, framed in a circle and a square, as he was seen by Leonardo da Vinci after Roman models.

Distorted, in order to adapt him to a freakish frame. The reality created by man is probably even more freakish than this drawing.

Source: Robert Guiducci, *La Societa Impazzita, Rizzoli, Milan (1980)*.

penetrating more deeply into the soil that we are unconsciously preparing each day. *Homo sapiens* is no longer what he used to be, or what we imagined he was. The allegory on page 124 is an attempt to convey that thought. The vision of a being of harmonious proportions perfectly suited to the natural environment, which Leonardo da Vinci bequeathed to us, is here placed beside a modern being, deformed and trapped in an environment that has been capriciously transformed. These distortions are becoming worse. And the more we grow in power and pride, the more probable and painful will be our downfall.

If the first and ultimate cause of our predicament lies within ourselves, then it is similarly up to us to restore our inner equilibrium and in that way to bring a fruitful harmony to our small corner of the Universe. It is, in fact, up to us to direct our thoughts and our actions so as to derive reasonable benefit from our labors, and not be crushed by them.

Yes, the problem lies within ourselves, not outside us. Therefore, it is within ourselves that we must seek solutions and the path of our salvation on Earth.

PART II.
THE STRAIGHT AND NARROW PATHS TO RENAISSANCE

THE DECISIVE DECADE

The Club of Rome Opens the Debate

To give due credit to The Club of Rome, one must recall that, even at the time of its founding in 1968, it saw clearly the basic outlines of the problems comprising the predicament that imperils the human future at the height of our knowledge and power. The first of its messages to the public at large was the report already mentioned, *The Limits to Growth*, published in 1972. Using available data and simple logic understandable to all, this report launched a direct attack on the complacency of industrial society. It argued that economic growth at all costs, at exponential rates, cannot be an end in itself. Such growth is bound to lead society to a disastrous collision with the limits and constraints of both natural and human systems. It was a courageous stand, defying the myth of material growth and challenging the tenets of the consumer society. For that reason, the book was condemned as heretical and scandalous, and it triggered an avalanche of criticism and protest. It was, nevertheless, a necessary and salutary warning.

Today, few people dare to defend the indiscriminate growth that was fashionable in the 'sixties. In 1979, even so conservative an economist and political leader as Valéry Giscard d'Estaing, then the President of France, declared:

"It has always been my feeling that the consumer society did not suit either France or the French. It laid waste a part of our coasts, our mountains, our cities, our way of life, our culture; it caused tremendous havoc. I think that the austere society we are aiming toward is basically better adapted to France ..."*

The debate opened by The Club of Rome on this subject, as well as on the world problematique and other issues related to the great human alternatives, soon snowballed. It was expressed in thousands of ways that I have no time to mention here. Meanwhile, the reports to The Club of Rome have grown in number. They are inspired by the purpose of The Club of Rome, which is to help reverse the current tendency towards decline in human affairs. For the reader desiring more information, those reports published to date are listed on the boxes on pages 129 and 130. Hundreds of other books and thousands of essays related to, or inspired by, these reports have appeared in a number of languages.

The arguments posed in the preceding pages are addressed to the same purpose. They point out several things, of which one of the most important is that our generations seem to have lost *the sense of the whole*. From all points of view, this loss represents a backward step, an unfortunate involution —especially since it has occurred at the very moment when many systems, old and new, are expanding and intertwining, thus deepening the complexity of the great metasystem of the world which gives humanity, willy-nilly, a substantial unity. A sense of the global and of universal harmony, which is characteristic to philosophical and religious thought and is the eternal quest of science, has also become an indispensable basis for

---

*Quoted in *Paris-Match* in September 1979.

Reports To The Club Of Rome

Donella H. Meadows, Dennis L. Meadows, Jorgen Randers, and William W. Behrens III, *The Limits to Growth,* Universe Books, New York and New American Library, New York (paperback edition), 1972.

Mihajlo D. Mesarovic and Eduard Pestel, *Mankind at the Turning Point,* E.P. Dutton, New York and New American Library, New York (paperback edition), 1974.

Jan Tinbergen (Coordinator), *Reshaping the International Order,* E.P. Dutton, New York and New American Library, New York (paperback edition), 1976.

Dennis Gabor and Umberto Colombo, *Beyond the Age of Waste,* Pergamon Press, New York, 1978.

Ervin Laszlo, *Goals for Mankind,* E.P. Dutton, New York and New American Library, New York (paperback edition), 1978.

Thierry de Montbrial, *Energy: The Countdown,* Pergamon Press, New York, 1979.

James W. Botkin, Mahdi Elmandjra, and Mircea Malitza, *No Limits to Learning,* Pergamon Press, New York, 1979.

Maurice Guernier, *Tiers-Monde: Trois Quarts du Monde,* Dunod, Paris, 1980. (No English edition)

Orio Giarini, *Dialogue on Wealth and Welfare,* Pergamon Press, New York, 1980.

Bohdan Hawrylyshyn, *Road Maps to the Future,* Pergamon Press, Oxford, 1980.

Companion Volumes

Aurelio Peccei, *The Chasm Ahead,* Macmillan Publishing Co., New York, 1969.

Dennis L. Meadows and Donella H. Meadows (editors), *Toward Global Equilibrium,* Wright-Allen Press, Inc., Cambridge, Massachusetts, 1973.

Aurelio Peccei, *Quale Futuro?,* Mondadori, Milan, 1974. (No English edition).

Aurelio Peccei, *The Human Quality,* Pergamon Press, New York, 1977.

Ervin Laszlo, *The Inner Limits of Mankind,* Pergamon Press, Oxford, England, 1978.

Alexander King, *The State of the Planet,* Pergamon International Library, Oxford, England, 1980.

informed political action. That sense must be restored to present-day society.

In other words, we should consider it obvious that, in order to approach fundamental questions — such as, for example, the possible outcomes of the Arab-Israeli conflict, the real alternatives for the development of Europe, Latin America, or Japan, the national goals that the United States can set for itself, whatever its administration, or the best means of educating the young — we must see them in the dynamic context of the socio-political evolution of the world. And, in order to combat the causes of famine, or the more recent phenomena of civil violence, terrorism, highjacking, and drug proliferation, we must seek their roots deep within the disorder and malfunction of contemporary global and national societies; we must consider them as individual parts of a broader problematique; and we must conceive their solutions as one aspect of restoring general order. All the more reason, therefore, if we are to perceive the complexity of the human predicament itself and grasp its true significance, for us to examine the human condition as a whole today, and its likely future development.

In this view, it is clear that to speak of the human being — the origin of all our problems and the foundation of all our hopes — only in terms of immediate or material needs, or of limited aspects of political or social life, is an unpardonable error. Pope John Paul II has emphasized this fact repeatedly, with the full weight of his authority. For example, in his address to UNESCO in June 1980, he stated that there is "a fundamental dimension which is capable of shaking to their very foundations the systems on which the whole of humanity is built and of liberating human existence, both individual and collective, from the dangers which threaten it. This fundamental dimension is man, man in his wholeness, man who lives at one and the same time in the sphere of material values and in that of spiritual values." In order to consider the fullness of the human personality, with all its needs and aspirations, we ought to ask ourselves whether and to what extent men and women are able to satisfy them and to reach their individual self-fulfillment — and also whether the human race has not become too numerous for all its offspring to develop their natural potential in this way. After all that has been said, the reader may be uncertain in answering this last question.

The Club of Rome realized that a sense of the global whole must be restored to our minds if we are to make a reliable diagnosis of the ills of humanity and find appropriate remedies. It is in some measure thanks to its efforts that progress has recently been made in this direction. The nature of certain difficulties is now better understood. We are beginning to connect the economy with ecology, security problems with social problems, the energy crisis with past political errors, and a given event in one corner of the globe with what is happening in another.

The Club of Rome also realized that our generations, swollen with pride in our technological triumphs, must regain *the sense of human responsibilities* that I have already mentioned. On this point, let me digress briefly.

For some time now, the perception of these responsibilities has motivated a number of organizations and small voluntary groups of concerned citizens which have mushroomed all over to respond to the demands of new situations or to change whatever is not going right in society. These groups are now legion. They arose sporadically on the most varied fronts and with different aims. They comprise peace movements, supporters of national liberation, and advocates of women's rights and population control; defenders of minorities, human rights, and civil liberties; apostles of "technology with a human face" and the humanization of work; social workers and activists for social change; ecologists, friends of the Earth or of animals; defenders of consumer rights; non-violent protesters; conscientious objectors, and many others. These groups are usually small but, should the occasion arise, they can mobilize a host of men and women, young and old, inspired by a profound sense of the common good and by moral obligations which, in their eyes, are more important than all others.

They form a kind of popular army, actual or potential, with a function comparable to that of the antibodies generated to restore normal conditions in a biological organism that is diseased or attacked by pathogenic agents. The existence of so many spontaneous organizations and groups testifies to the vitality of our societies, even in the midst of the crisis they are undergoing. Means will have to be found one day to consolidate their scattered efforts in order to direct them towards strategic objectives.

After this digression, it is appropriate to mention another important quality that The Club of Rome is trying to evoke. This is *the consciousness of the species*. This primordial and instinctive force, which is the mainspring of the living world, has in a way been diminished by the artificial and sheltered environment we have created for ourselves. It has also been weakened by the competition of two somewhat abstract products of our "civilization," namely "national consciousness" and "class consciousness." The former has been exacerbated by the myths of sovereignty that have already been mentioned. As for class consciousness, it was born in industrialized nations as a result of the struggles of the oppressed classes to redress the balance of a blatantly unjust society. More recently, it has been revived and transposed to the global context in the form of the ideal of a new and more just international economic order. It inspires the struggle of what Arnold Toynbee has called "the external proletariat" against the exploitation to which it is subjected by the wealthy countries.

New facts have now intervened to reawaken our consciousness of the species. On one hand, people are worried about the recrudescence of traditional nationalism, a degenerate form of national consciousness that is leading to serious international frictions. On the other hand, class struggles are turning out to be increasingly costly and sterile. Even the disinherited are discovering that, beyond the social and economic injustices they are suffering, there is perhaps an even more dreadful apocalypse hanging over the whole world, of which they would be the first victims. The new perception of common dangers and of a certain community of interests, in fact, is tending to highlight the advantages of a solidarity that extends beyond all political and social frontiers, and to facilitate a resurgence of the consciousness of the species at a moment when the whole human race must face up to decisive challenges to its future.

The foundations for further progress have thus been laid. The Club of Rome is nevertheless preparing to widen the debate still more. While firmly maintaining its universal view, it will place particular emphasis on *the problems and prospects of human development*. This will be its most absorbing and important enterprise. While objective indicators point to a progressive and accelerated worsening of the situation on all other fronts, the human element seems to be recovering. After a phase of materialistic exaltation, followed by one of fatalistic bewilderment, people seem to be realizing that the advancement of humanity — of every nation, of every individual — is of paramount importance. This is a starting point that can lead to a positive evolution. We are becoming aware, slowly but surely, of a disconcerting reality that is sweeping us along in its wake, and are rejecting the unhappy fate it implies; we are beginning to react, to place our hopes on what we ourselves, working together, are capable of accomplishing.

This is the state of humanity at the threshold of the 'eighties — deeply concerned, very ill-prepared, but with a growing awareness of the need to revise its positions. Everything will depend on whether we are able to recognize the realities, and apply the full range of our intelligence and skills accordingly.

Last Chance for Humankind?

At this point, we know a great deal. We know that, even if the future cannot be predicted, it can, within certain limits and in broad outlines, be invented, modeled, fabricated; and that the invention of the future, although fundamental and vital, will be all the more difficult since it will have to be the collective effort of billions of people. We also know that the future defined by the projection of present conditions and trends can only be stormy and dark; and that the first thing we must do is to improve those conditions and reverse those trends at the earliest possible moment.

The indispensable invention, therefore, is that of learning how to create a situation in which the sum total of human activity and behavior today will produce a more favorable set of conditions tomorrow. And we also know that this must be a cultural evolution. In the case of other species, their genetic evolution has the task of adapting them biologically *a posteriori* to changes taking place in their environment; those that survive have proved that they have passed the test. Human cultural evolution, by contrast, must be *anticipatory* to allow us to survive amid the tumult of change for which we ourselves are continually responsible.

We have also asked ourselves many questions; and a number of them remain unanswered because their main purpose is to make us think. The moment has come now, however, to ask ourselves the final question: *Who must do what, and when, to prepare for the future?*

As to the question of *who must act*, there can be no doubt. To be effective, the cultural evolution of the human race must include everyone. Yet, not all individuals carry the same weight; and their respective influences on alternatives for the future are very different. The most deprived groups of people who are jammed together at the bottom of the social pyramid cannot even think of their own future; and, for that reason, they can contribute very little to the future of humankind. These are groups and, indeed, whole populations condemned to be nothing but *the unconscious slaves of the future*, prisoners of a future that others are to determine. I have already observed that such situations are no longer politically tolerable. In fact, one of the most urgent tasks is to give all these human beings on the margins of society a chance to participate in some way in its progress.

By contrast, firmly installed at the top of the pyramid are the classes and sectors of society who make the decisions that affect the course of all future events. To this portion of the pyramid also belong the military caste and the intelligentsia of scientists, economists, and intellectuals who advise, caution, or inspire the decision-makers. These demonstrably nearsighted officials decide the shape of things to come — they are thus *the myopic artificers of the future*. They have been improvident and ignorant in shaping the present, since they were unable either to predict or avoid the current predicament; and it is largely the fault of their mediocre performance that society is adrift, that humanity is on the decline. This same kind of decision maker is now in the process once again of betraying the hopes of the human race for tomorrow, because they do not seem to have learned any lessons and, preoccupied totally by the needs of the short term, are continuing to push events in the same direction as yesterday. Consequently, it is the mode of thinking and acting of these potentates and their grand viziers that must henceforth undergo the most drastic transformation.

But cultural advances at the pinnacle of society and rehabilitation of the amorphous masses at its base cannot have much effect if they are not reinforced by a reaffirmation of the value of the average citizen. *It is the people as a whole who are the true bearers of the future.* Their rise, and their awakening to a consciousness of the new human condition and the greater responsibilities it implies, are the pivots upon which the redirection of society depends. Moreover, it is the people far more than the ruling classes who bear the brunt of all the crises and who thus are more sensitive to the need for reform; it is the people who see more clearly the necessity of innovations that will guarantee more equality, more security, more peace. They are concerned; they feel that the basic tenets of society need to be restated; they are personally ready and open for an "acculturation" that will open up new horizons. They want to understand and to believe, to mature and to participate, to be and to become. The potential power of renewal is within them. It is they who represent the living source of a new culture, the hope for tomorrow.

Questions concerning the future, then, demand approaches that engage human society in all its parts and at all its levels, and at the same time accord people the principal role. The assignment of this principal role to the people is vital, for although the elite may have a valuable function as a vanguard, as prime movers or advance scouts, they may also abuse their privilege. History has witnessed many tyrants. Even now, there are a fair number of dictatorial regimes. A group of scientists may confront an ill-prepared society with discoveries that have unsettling and irreversible effects; and a mere handful of individuals can unleash the final holocaust. Only alert and vigilant citizens can prevent these errors of judgment or performance, and write the history of a future worth living. Furthermore, with the spread of education, mobility, information, and communications in a system in which everything depends on everything else, the structure of power is undergoing change; the people themselves are increasingly invested with greater responsibilities. Consequently, they find themselves facing the inevitable necessity of learning how to govern, and how to govern themselves.

The second part of the question is: *to do what?* We must realize that there are no magic formulas or ready-made plans for the future, nor any known remedies or precise norms to guide us, nor in fact any valid experiments on a smaller scale that can be applied on the global scale. *Everything must be invented anew in order to invent the future*, even the methods to be followed.

As I have already stated, the starting point must be a clear understanding of how the human condition is changing in our era. And this must be accompanied by the conviction that it is possible to formulate coherent plans for the future. Without this deep and reasoned conviction, such an exceptional undertaking is inconceivable.

To quote former President Giscard d'Estaing again, he was both right and wrong when, at the beginning of his seven-year term, he declared that "The world is unhappy; it is unhappy because it does not know where it is going and because it has a shrewd idea that if it did know, it would only discover that it is on its way to disaster."* He was right

---

* Ibid.

in his diagnosis, but wrong in suggesting there is no way out of the situation and also in making an implicit apology of ignorance for social ills. This book, by contrast, besides aiming to make people think, tries to introduce ideas to demonstrate that solutions — even though very difficult to imagine and still harder to implement — really do exist. *The trump cards of knowledge and power* on which the euphoria of the 'sixties was based are still in our hands, and are more important than ever. They constitute a formidable even if mixed patrimony, which is growing rapidly although in a disorderly way, and which is currently being utilized in a thoughtless, careless, and wasteful manner. It both can and must be put in order and used intelligently. In other words, we have both the possibility and duty to reach, if not the "optimization" of the use of all our knowledge and instruments of progress, then at least their "sub-optimization," instead of succumbing to — if I may be permitted such a word — the "quasi-pessimization" that exists at present.

Quite obviously, there are thousands of *things to do in all spheres*. Those that need to be done at a local and national level require decisions at those levels — which should, however, take account of the more general regional or global exigencies. In the following pages, I propose to deal only with imperatives at this higher level. And, in this connection, two preliminary observations seem appropriate.

The first concerns the approach to be chosen. It is an old truth that what is being observed may be important, but the point of view from which it is observed is no less important. If we continue to regard the world situation from certain viewpoints while excluding others, our perspective will be influenced and probably distorted; certain aspects will no doubt be missed; and the distant horizons will remain unclear. But that is precisely what is being done at the present time. *The points of entry we adopt to assess and cope with the problematique* are always the same: national interest, economic development, energy supply, or the balance of military power. This stereotyped approach may lead to gross errors of judgment. The complex of modern society's problems should, on the contrary, be examined from a number of vantage points, capable of providing as balanced an overall view as possible. The latter is the approach that I will continue to employ.

The second point is that one often hears it said that we know what must be done, but *what is lacking is the political will* to do it. That is partly true and I shall come back to it presently; but, quite frequently, it is nothing but an alibi. In fact, it happens that plans, programs, or projects that are excellent in themselves remain a dead letter not because of any lack of political will, but because to carry them out would require innovations in many other fields, and the new foundations on which they must depend are not being constructed. Devising valid solutions to problems more often than not demands, in fact, that we call into question the very bases of present-day society. And that effort is tacitly rejected, or not even discussed — for many reasons, often simply because it would challenge the dogma of national sovereignty, or at the very least its orthodox interpretation, and consequently would undermine the enormous privileges that have built up around it.

With that said, let us see what must be done. I will limit my discussion to *certain fundamental exigencies of a general nature that must guide all action*. They concern political and cultural imperatives that absolutely must be met if we want the world community to become more organic, mutually coherent, and more capable of beginning to build its future in a responsible manner.

Like everything else, these imperatives are interdependent and complex in themselves. They can nevertheless be summarized under three headings, in order of ascending importance, as follows:

- Implement global policies and strategies.
- Bring the world into governable condition.
- Learn how to govern the world — which presupposes learning how to govern ourselves.

To fulfill these unprecedented conditions, humanity will have to make a supreme, heroic effort and win a psychological victory over itself. We must be willing to admit to ourselves that we have brought about a disastrous state of affairs, at the very time when we believed we were moving toward our greatest triumphs. We will have to sacrifice principles and premises hallowed by experience; renounce certain attitudes that have been the very basis of our progress; abandon habits that have brought us well-being and comfort; and reverse judgments that have formed part of our conventional wisdom. And we must be frank and objective with ourselves. The credibility of the undertaking is essential. Our examination of the present must be rigorous, even brutal, and our studies of the future must conceal none of its potential difficulties and dangers; at the same time, they must point out clearly and honestly the real possibilities for recovery.

The third part of the question concerns the time factor. *When must humankind make this supreme effort?* Here too, as far as I am concerned, there is no doubt. The pressure of events is pitiless. Even though the processes of renewal will be relatively slow, and the fear and distrust engendered by change or innovation will not be quickly dispelled, the fundamental imperatives that I have mentioned cannot wait. We must restore order on board Spaceship Earth before things get totally out of hand.

If the time at our disposal to carry out this massive undertaking is very short, how long is it, in fact? From now til the end of the century? I believe that we can count on even less than that. *The decade of the 'eighties will be decisive.* It is also probable that the first part of this decade may influence the history of humankind into the very distant future.

We are living in a kind of *grace period*, during which our species still has a good chance of redressing its hazardous situation. But if we miss this opportunity, we will probably never again have the possibility to keep the descending spiral of our decline from becoming a precipitous downfall.

Global Policies and Strategies

The first basic requirement, if we are to escape from the present crisis, is *to adopt a series of policies and strategies that respond to the global interests of humankind.* It must be borne in mind, however, that at present and for as long as society is organized as a system of sovereign states, human activities will continue to be regulated at the national level. But to harmonize more than 150 selfish nationalisms in a serious and constructive manner is almost impossible. Each country pursues its objectives according to its own criteria and its own "sacred" national interest, quite independently of what other countries are doing, if not in direct opposition to them.

On the other hand, the nation-state, the keystone of the entire global political edifice, cannot be changed for the moment. The problem therefore is how to make this same nation-state evolve so that it becomes a positive element for the global future. It is only common sense not to launch a frontal attack on it without careful advance preparation. The urgency of attaining our goal must not lead us into ill-advised premature or imprudent action.

First of all, we must create *a consciousness of the imperative of global solidarity.* A process of education and self-education, and a movement of ideas and opinions, are necessary to this end. The arguments that I have advanced here should be elaborated, debated, criticized, corrected, confirmed. If the public is to be able and willing to accept and support a substantial change in policies, it must be in no doubt about what the planetary realities are. In fact, these will ultimately be more convincing than preconceived ideas that quickly become outdated, and people will eventually accept the fact that the good of the whole world is indispensable for the good of all nations and of their own nation in particular.

In parallel with this psychological "de-sovereignization" of the nation-state, the strongest nations ought to set an example by unilaterally renouncing certain specific aspects of their sovereignty. But, even in the absence of such initiatives, advantage must be taken of all possible opportunities to proceed pragmatically in the creation of what might be called *a global social system* — to take its place along with natural ecosystems and the technical metasystem. A considerable network of established international agreements already exists, not to protect direct national interests but for more generous ends. The network must be reinforced.

One means of doing so is through development of

regional communities, of which I will have more to say; another is through *voluntary coalitions of nations to achieve goals of general interest.* I have dealt with this matter more fully in my book *The Human Quality.** I merely want to note here in passing that, although not systematic, such an affirmation of ideas and establishment of new international structures will, once undertaken, gather its own momentum. It will progressively bring about changes in international behavior and law as well as in world public opinion — each of which in turn will facilitate the more profound evolutionary changes I have mentioned above. What has happened in the United Nations in this regard is very instructive.

The United Nations system is generally considered to be overgrown, very bureaucratic, quite ineffective, and excessively politicized. And yet, it is the United Nations, the forum of sovereign states, which has gone beyond the intentions of the myopic defenders of the primacy of the nation-state in helping, more than any other body, to stimulate an awareness of global problems. This result has been achieved, above all, thanks to the *major international conferences* organized by the United Nations during the 'seventies, which are listed on page 145. It is not so much the conferences themselves, which have served as both assembly and marketplace for thousands of people from every continent to expound their beliefs, that have been important. Nor has it been the speeches made by delegates, mainly for the benefit of their distant national audiences, nor the tens of thousands of pages of documents that they supposedly have studied but that were, in fact,

---

* Aurelio Peccei, *The Human Quality* (Oxford, England: Pergamon International Library, 1977).

The Principal Global Conferences Of The United Nations

1972 — United Nations Conference on the Human Environment, Stockholm

1974 — United Nations World Population Conference, Bucharest

1975 — Second General Conference of the United Nations Industrial Development Organization (UNIDO), Lima

1976 — United Nations Conference on Human Settlements, Vancouver

1977 — World Conference for Action Against Apartheid, Lagos

— United Nations Conference on Desertification, Nairobi

1978 — World Conference to Combat Racism and Racial Discrimination, Geneva

— United Nations Conference on Technical Co-operation Among Developing Countries, Buenos Aires

1979 — United Nations Conference on Science and Technology for Development, Vienna

— World Conference on Agrarian Reform and Rural Development, Rome

1980 — World Conference on the United Nations Decade for Women: Equality, Development, and Peace, Copenhagen

read only by a few officials here and there. What has been important is the atmosphere of concern that these conferences have succeeded in creating around a series of grave and urgent global problems. These go beyond any challenges humanity has faced up to now, and no people or nation can handle them alone; we must confront them together as quickly as possible. The U.N. conferences were a first step in that direction.

There is, on the other hand, an abundance of ideas about plans, programs, projects, and various instruments and institutions that ought to be brought into play. Proposals, some good and others less good, are constantly being made by United Nations agencies themselves or by others — especially by the non-governmental organizations that I have called the antibodies of their societies. It goes without saying that the proposals of the latter are those that contain the greatest leaven of new ideas. Gradually, as some of these suggestions and recommendations are put into practice, other bolder ones will come along to reinforce them. Of all the proposals waiting to be implemented, I will mention only two, which were outlined by comprehensive reports presented by private, independent, and multicultural working groups. They refer specifically to the North-South relationship, but their general aim is to help the world move towards a fairer and more satisfactory organization.

The first set of interrelated proposals was presented in a report to The Club of Rome completed in 1976 under the direction of the great Dutch economist Jan Tinbergen. The title of the report is *Reshaping the International Order*, but it is better known as the RIO Report. It covers a wide range of subjects and proposes a vast number of measures necessary to reduce the inequalities of the world progressively and to guarantee "a decent life and modest prosperity for all citizens." And it has the courage to point out what a long, arduous, and complex undertaking this will be. Its main recommendations are arranged in three distinct packages of proposals for comprehensive negotiation:

- Proposals aimed at reducing gross inequities in the distribution of world income and economic opportunities;
- Proposals to ensure more harmonious growth of the global economic system; and
- Proposals to provide the beginnings of a global planning system.

The second document, still very topical, was presented in February 1980 under the title *North-South: A Program for Survival** and is known as the Brandt Commission Report, from the name of Willy Brandt, who presided over the commission that produced it. It is oriented primarily towards problems of economic development. For this reason, it has been criticized for being one-dimensional, and for not giving sufficient attention to ecology or to the individual. Its recommendations are also very complex and detailed, and were partly inspired by the RIO Report and by other works of recent years. *North-South* presents an emergency program for 1980-85 under four major headings:

- A large-scale transfer of resources to developing countries;
- An international energy strategy;

---

* Willy Brandt, *North-South: A Program for Survival* (Cambridge, Massachusetts: MIT Press, 1980).

- A global food program; and
- A start on major reforms in the international economic system.

In my opinion, the most interesting aspect of the Brandt Commission Report is that it attempts to put an end, by political means, to the stalemate between North and South, by translating the mutual interests of the rich and poor countries into active forms of collaboration. With this end in view, it proposes one or more North-South summit meetings. These would have to take an appropriate form and include, if possible, the participation of representatives of the East — who for the moment have not accepted the invitation. At this writing, plans have been completed for the first meeting, to take place on October 22-23, 1981 in Cancún, Mexico. Those participating will be about ten chiefs or state or heads of government of countries representing the North, and a slightly larger number from the South. Mexican President José López Portillo and Austrian Chancellor Bruno Kreisky will be its co-presidents and Canadian Prime Minister Pierre Elliott Trudeau will play an important part in it.

The quality of these men is such that one can be certain that a great effort will be made to spare the world even graver crises. But the agenda will be difficult and complex. One need only cite the necessity of reducing national selfishness and of carrying out the institutional reforms necessary to make existing international organizations, or others that may be created, more responsive to the realities and demands of our time.

The concept of North-South summits is excellent — provided that the leading participants realize clearly what the world expects of them. It expects that they will meet to study the alternatives and options open to humankind, not as negotiators, each serving the interests of his own country, but as *partners who must establish together the equitable contribution that each of them should make to the common global good.* All who are capable of contributing must make a maximum effort to foster this spirit among those who have the task of preparing, or participating in, these meetings. For if these great summits were to turn out, on the contrary, to be more or less inconclusive, routine affairs, the negative psychological and political repercussions would be incalculable in a world already in a precarious state.

The plain, unvarnished truth is that humanity is not satisfied with its leaders. It is right. It senses danger, feels on its neck the hot breath of menacing events drawing ever closer. No matter whether there are summit meetings or not, whether the resolutions passed by the United Nations are more or less rhetorical, or whether the eventual compromises reached during global negotiations are drafted in one form or another, the human race wants to know where it is going. It is tired of statesmen who can never find a way to agree on essentials, tired of national and international bureaucracies that have a talent for identifying all our difficulties and sweeping issues under the rug, but cannot find a single solution to our basic problems. It has the feeling that the moment has come *to demand an act of leadership from those who hold power in the world.* Humanity wants someone from among those to whom it has delegated decision-making authority to rise above the struggle, to offer guidance towards a situation in which it can find some direction, and to state clearly what price in sweat and sacrifice, even in blood and tears, it must pay in order to escape from its present predicament.

To go back to the voluntary coalitions mentioned in preceding pages, which are the peaceful equivalent of military alliances, such an act of leadership could be the decision taken freely and collectively by a group of states to unite, not merely to sign documents, but to achieve together, on a practical level, a constructive goal beyond the sphere of any individual nation. The member states would commit themselves in effect to adopt jointly, in the common interest and towards a higher good, certain long-term norms and policies — thus at the same time laying the foundations of a new order on a transnational scale.

There are several sectors and problems in which the technical details are very fully developed and the consensus of opinion fairly broad, and others in which the needs are very obvious, which therefore lend themselves to the formation of such coalitions. The box on page 151 gives an idea of some initiatives that might be considered. It would not be necessary for all the states that ought to be natural partners in one or other initiative to join immediately. The main thing would be to make a start, and to keep the door open for new members.

To conclude this long discussion, I would add that good work is under way in defining the frames of reference and the necessary cognitive bases for coordinated regional and global strategies and policies. Very useful to this end is the report to The Club of Rome by my colleague Bohdan Hawrylyshyn, which analyzes the efficiency of the major national societies and their modes of operation in this phase of transition towards the future.*

Among other more specific studies, I think that *Global*

---

* Bohdan Hawrylyshyn, *Road Maps to the Future* (Oxford, England: Pergamon International Library, 1980).

Examples of Policies and Strategies In the Global Interest

- *World Conservation Strategy*. This was the subject of the detailed study already mentioned (see page 74), which offers concrete proposals in a whole series of sectors. Its aim is to facilitate the achievement of lasting economic development based on good management and the conservation of living resources.
- *Elimination of hunger and malnutrition*. The Universal Declaration solemnly adopted to this end at the 1974 World Food Conference has not really been put into practice. But the FAO and the World Food Council have drawn up very clear and detailed plans and convincing strategies that are now awaiting political decisions. The aim must be the wise use, on both national and international levels, of all available resources of soil, energy, water, technology, capital, and climate, and the comprehensive development of mechanisms necessary to bring these Biblical scourges to an end once and for all.
- *Multinational energy policies*. These ought to be adopted by common agreement between producing and importing countries, at least on the regional level. The aim must be to create a spirit of partnership and orderly procedures to guide the transition from the former period of abundant and cheap energy to the new period of scarce and expensive energy. These procedures must reward the conservation of energy by all possible means, combining appropriate development of all available sources, while assuring maximum protection of the environment.
- *Research on planning*. The objectives and activities of the various nations and regions must be mutually coherent in a planet with limited space and scarce re-

sources. The aim must be to perfect measures and practical techniques for joint consultation and planning for the medium and long term.

• Other examples could be cited in the most varied spheres — reform of the international monetary system, regulation of international money markets, technical measures for disarmament, disarmament itself, control or abolition of the international traffic in arms, etc.

• It must be recognized that agreements of this kind are extremely difficult to achieve. But, without them, life in our world will become even more difficult.

*2000** deserves to be singled out. Completed in July 1980, this is a comprehensive study of global trends in population, resources, and environment through the year 2000, prepared at the request of the President of the United States by thirteen different agencies and departments of the U.S. government, under the direction of another colleague, Gerald O. Barney. The purpose of the project is to improve the government's capacity for long-range analysis and planning, as a guide for current decision-making. According to the report, the existing capacity is now far from meeting the needs of senior policy officials. Indeed, *Global 2000* states candidly that "the executive agencies of the U.S. Government are not now capable of presenting the President with internally consistent projections of world trends in population, resources, and environment for the next two decades."** And I fear that the government of

---

* Gerald O. Barney, Study Director, *The Global 2000 Report to the President: Entering the Twenty-First Century,* 3 vols. (Washington, D.C.: U.S. Government Printing Office, 1980).

** *Ibid., 2: 454.*

the United States is by no means unique in this regard. The *Global 2000* initiative exemplifies the kind of concerns that are beginning to penetrate into the most advanced government circles; it is encouraging that several other countries — including Canada, China, Spain, and Japan — are in process of studying and adapting *Global 2000* to their own national requirements.

Global 2000 was followed six months later, in January 1981, by a companion report, prepared under the direction of the Department of State and the President's Council for Environmental Quality, entitled *Global Future: Time to Act.* This latter report identifies the action implications of *Global 2000* in 13 major interrelated issue areas, ranging from international development to energy conservation, population policy to water resources, and tropical forests to public education and institutional change. These two recent U.S. government studies are under active consideration by the American administration, and have already led, among other things, to the formation in the private sector of a new consortium of more than 50 U.S. organizations concerned with global trends in resources, population, and environment, and the improvement of U.S. national foresight capacity. Called the Global Tomorrow Coalition, this consortium includes groups whose total combined membership exceeds five million Americans. It is an example of the kind of future-oriented non-governmental body that is developing in many countries.

In conclusion, we have begun to see the emergence of the imperative that the outmoded values and tribal behavior of the nation-state must be abandoned in favor of a broad sense of global solidarity. This imperative must now be catalyzed into effective political action. To achieve this end, those who are most sensitive to the need for change must continue to exert pressure on centers of decision, so that plans for the good of all humankind may be pursued even at the risk of some sacrifices at the national level. In the end, the balance sheet can only be positive. Restoring the planet to good order, assuring that it can sustain the entire immense population that will soon inhabit it, establishing institutions and policies consonant with these objectives — these are not only the highest enterprise to which we can contribute, but also the best investment of our time, our talents, and our hopes.

Two Political Imperatives

The paths to salvation will not be easy. On the contrary, they are likely to be rough and tortuous by-ways, strewn with obstacles. And it will be necessary to try out several of them before finding those that offer the best chances of progress. The first fundamental requirement to facilitate the search is the one we have just noted, namely, beginning to think and act with a global outlook. Inseparable from it, however, is the second fundamental requirement of *assuring the governability of the human system*, which now, as we have seen, is blocked mainly by East-West tensions and by the North-South structural imbalance. The elimination of these two obstacles, therefore, is the central political imperative of our time. They are interrelated in various ways but, to simplify the discussion, let us examine them separately.

As far as the East-West axis is concerned, I would say that the stabilization of the present situation, détente, peaceful coexistence, or even the elimination of tensions are no longer enough. We cannot be content merely to improve the political and psychological climate. The global situation is so bad, and is so rapidly growing worse on all fronts, that coordinated, large-scale interventions are necessary to reverse these trends. *Active East-West collaboration has become indispensable.* Despite the differing policies and opposing ideologies of East and West, and despite whatever reasons may justify the current tensions, I believe such collaboration is possible. Let us briefly examine the terms of the question.

The wealth and productivity of what we are pleased to call the free Western, or Westernized, democracies, are far superior to those of the socialist countries. Even if we consider only the United States, Canada, and the European Community — excluding Japan and the other countries of the OECD — their combined gross national products comprise almost half the world total, and are about three times that of the Soviet bloc. The latter is weakened by the Achilles heel of agriculture, and is incapable of producing enough food to satisfy the growing needs of its population. But, behind the shield of the Soviet Union, which apparently devotes roughly 12 percent of its own gross national product to armaments, the Soviet bloc has managed to achieve military equality with, if not superiority over, the West. It also has the strength of those who are willing to sacrifice the present for the future. Furthermore, it is the socialist regimes that are advocating change in the present world order; more often than not, the initiative is theirs. It is they who have more numerous friends in a world of discontent — and their friends are more committed and more disciplined than those of the West. The two groups, represented by the Warsaw Pact and the Atlantic Alliance, are thus ultimately balanced in their ability to neutralize each other. But their deadlock has a paralyzing influence on the world system.

While understanding this situation, the leaders on both sides keep hoping to outwit their adversaries and to gain maximum advantage over them — without risking any direct military confrontation. They know that a test of strength might degenerate against their wishes into an exchange of nuclear attacks, which either of the two super-powers is equipped to unleash, but against which neither has a viable defense. At the moment, the balance of terror serves as a deterrent, but no one knows what may happen from one day to the next; and in any case, this is an exceedingly expensive state of affairs. I am convinced that both sides have now reached the point at which, if a suitable opportunity should arise, they would be ready to explore other less dangerous and more constructive means to promote their interests.

In order to sound out this possibility, I have had direct or indirect contacts in the camps of East and West for more than three years now, and I think I have good grounds to assert that their state of mind is much more mature than official policies would indicate. The continuity of dialogue has been interrupted by the Soviet thrust into Afghanistan. Once a more or less "satisfactory" situation has been restored there, and if no other major international disruption occurs — in short, when life is back to "normal" again — this delicate web of contacts can be resumed in appropriate forms. Not only are these contacts even more necessary than before, but a number of people are now convinced that the world crisis makes it incumbent upon us all to look for emergency exits before it is too late.

As I have already stressed, time is working against all of us; the next very few years may be decisive, in a negative sense. It is therefore an absolute must to mobilize the combined efforts of East and West to help the human system regain strength and hope before its demographic, ecological, economic, and social conditions degrade any further, making its recovery even more difficult. In a word, we must hasten, and profit by, any possible openings — and endeavor to create favorable opportunities — because *to achieve East-West cooperation only by the end of the decade may, indeed, be too late.*

The plan once was, and could again be, very simple. The process of priming East-West cooperation would start with informal meetings at a very high level between individuals who hold positions of great responsibility in various spheres of activity, but who would act in a personal capacity. They would compare information and opinions on world problems. They would promote joint studies, as objective and unprejudiced as possible, to clarify areas of disagreement and illuminate the most complex of these problems. They would then restate the most important questions according to the dynamics of the present and the prospects for the future at this exceptional turning point in history. On these bases, conclusions would be drawn with regard to the policies that humanity in general — and East and West, or other human groups, in particular — could or should adopt to redress situations of common interest.

The aim would be to make *a joint global evaluation of the state of the planet*, and the ways in which East and West believe it can and must be improved. In that manner, it ought to be possible to work out together, as realistically as possible, a series of overall scenarios for the future. Or, it could be decided at least what alternative futures can derive from the present on the basis of various packages of national and international policies that the main protagonists might adopt from now on.

The core idea is that the exercise would lead to a spontaneous convergence of preferences for certain desirable futures and the unqualified rejection of others; and, more important still, that such a global vision of the future would allow East and West to see more precisely the broad areas in which they have interests and goals in common, which can be better served when they coordinate their policies rather than act separately at cross-purposes. It also seems logical that many of the problems that mesmerize us at the moment and have become symbols of the poisoned East-West relationship — for example, the politico-military situation in the Persian Gulf, fear of a nuclear surprise attack, or the constant subversive activities by one side against the adversary's positions somewhere in the world — would lose much of their virulence, even their entire significance. A different kind of relationship focusing on economic, scientific, and cultural cooperation would move to the forefront. And, gradually, other positive steps would be taken until it became possible, even natural, to seek together to define in principle the outlines of *joint global management of certain key human affairs.*

Even if I like to think of myself as an idealist, my forty years of experience as an industrial manager have taught me to keep my feet on the ground. Yet I am firmly convinced that it is possible to reconcile Soviet views with those of Europe and America, as I have just said, with regard to a number of major world problems, and to launch a common search for possible solutions. In this connection, it may be useful to respond immediately to the easy criticism that this would lead to intolerable domination by the superpowers over the rest of the world. One answer is that they already dominate it to a great degree. Furthermore, scholars and researchers from other com-

re than similarities, can provide a meeting-
ource of mutual development both within
nd in relations among them.

out saying that the decision to follow the
urse should strengthen the autonomous
the South, and the conclusion of treaties of
tercommunity agreements should not be
titute for, or a pretext to reduce, aid and
nological, industrial, financial, and com-
oration on the part of the North. On the
North-South relations will be ever more
nd the community solution should make it
k these ties more broadly to longer-term
developed countries would thus be in a
ke more efficient use of the means provided
n the basis of wider and more open competi-
le pernicious influence of political and pri-
which find rather easy ground in bilateral

0, The Club of Rome, along with two
izations — one from the United Nations,
d the other from the Third World, CEES-
nsored an international conference at the
s headquarters in New York. Its aim was to
ssibilities and advantages of a regional/in-
ther than national, approach to the much
w International Economic Order — which
be *a new world order*. Although the United
forum of sovereign national states, the con-

s Institute for Training and Research, in New York,
conomic and Social Studies of the Third World, in

munities could and should be associated as soon as possible in this East-West initiative. And, at any rate, a certain
assurance would be gained that the danger of confrontation between the superpowers would be reduced at least for
a time. The main advantage, however, would be the cultural, political, and psychological impact of the fact that the
great powers of the world should be discussing openly, in
front of all the other countries and world public opinion,
not their unedifying differences, but the real alternatives
for humankind. That would be well worth the risk that they
might possibly derive a few extra benefits for themselves in
the process.

China and Japan have been left out of this argument
because, following the two world wars that broke out in
Europe, the epicenter of great potential conflicts remains
the strategic area between the Atlantic and Indian Oceans.
The world is threatened by mounting rivalries in this critical staging area. All the same, there is no doubt that the two
great nations of the Far East ought to participate at an
appropriate time in these exchanges of ideas and studies of
a global scope; and this for another and even more essential
reason. They are already offering the world an admirable
example of good will and wisdom in their reciprocal relations. After long periods of separation, confrontation, and
struggle, they have embarked on a course of unprecedented
collaboration. Their contribution may be as precious as is
their example.

One may even think of creating in this way a kind of
round table on the human prospect. This round table might
become a permanent feature of the world to come and,
without having any official character, would certainly
influence government policies. At that point, it ought to
open itself to all other communities, and become universal.

I maintain, however, that it is up to the East and West to take the initiative under the specific terms I have indicated. The reason is not only that it is they who have the greatest influence on the course of world events; it is also that, conceived in this way, a bold departure to "another future" has, in my view, good chances of becoming a viable one. Is it not, then, primarily for the great nations of East and West to abandon their sterile and danger-laden antagonisms and show that they are determined to enter the future in a manner corresponding to their immense capacities and their unparalleled world responsibilities? If they demonstrate leadership, others will follow.

The other vital political imperative at a time of growing planetary interdependence concerns the asymmetric structure of the North-South relationship. Under present conditions, as I have noted, the global system is intrinsically unbalanced and the world is absolutely ungovernable. In order to make human affairs manageable, *it is essential for the South to be integrated organically into the global system.* And, to attain this goal, the South first of all must both help itself and receive help to arise from its present state of structural inferiority. So long as it remains fragmented and amorphous, the South will be hopelessly condemned not only to subservience to the North, but also to inefficiency in acting in its own interests and in those of humanity as a whole.

Many things are necessary to meet this exigency of change. However, mindful of the analysis on the preceding pages, I shall insist on only one fundamental step, which is a prerequisite for most of the others. The people who are struggling for existence under such difficult conditions in the South of the planet should realize that they must adopt models of political and economic aggregation that will

allow them to organiz[...]
adequate scope and [...]
remain forever depen[...]
the possibility of carr[...]
giants of the North; [...]
within; or blossoming[...]
genius. The post-feud[...]
in Europe more than t[...]
quate for the accomp[...]
colonial era.

Along with a numb[...]
ers from the Third V[...]
solution at present, w[...]
regional communities[...]
ment prepared for Th[...]
writes that these comr[...]
boring nations linked[...]
common destiny, whi[...]
losing their nationa[...]
together with the prob[...]
power to solve: the g[...]
lems, and those of th[...]
regional communities[...]
structures between th[...]
Albert Tévoédjrè, on[...]
personalities, adds to[...]
within the North-Sot[...]
solidarity between pt[...]
range of topics, and n[...]
would be "an organic[...]

---

* Albert Tévoédjrè, *La F*[...]
Les Editions Ouvrieres, 19[...]

which, even[...]
point and a[...]
communitie[...]

It goes w[...]
community [...]
developmen[...]
solidarity o[...]
seen as a st[...]
economic, t[...]
mercial coll[...]
contrary, th[...]
indispensabl[...]
possible to [...]
goals. The [...]
position to r[...]
by the Nortł[...]
tion, outside[...]
vate interest[...]
relations.

In May [...]
research org[...]
UNITAR,*[...]
TEM** — s[...]
United Nati[...]
explore the [...]
terregional,[...]
anticipated l[...]
would, in fac[...]
Nations is th[...]

---

* United Nati[...]
** Center fo[...]
Mexico City.

sensus was almost unanimous. The whole world is seeking a way out of the impasse reached in both the North-South dialogue and the debate on the need for a new world order. The idea of a regional/interregional approach has therefore arrived just in time.

This possibility must be thoroughly explored. If one could organize humankind on an intercommunity basis, there would be many advantages apart from those already mentioned. They are quite obvious. Only about a dozen or fifteen regional systems or sub-systems would need to be interlinked, and not a number ten times as large of more or less sovereign states. The virus of national sovereignty would be partly neutralized. Each community — of continental size, comparable to that of China and India — would have a much better possibility than would individual states of reconciling the competing demands of self-reliance and interdependence within its large and varied domain. Nations belonging to the same community would be obliged to resolve their differences within the community framework without disturbing overall global relations, as happens constantly today. The world would become more stable; it would be less concerned with and worried about the present; it could devote itself more to the future. Its development —social, political, and economic — would be largely freed from the influence of narrow, selfish nationalisms. And, finally, it could be guided by *a true dialogue of civilizations*, each unfolding in its own natural area, each making its original contribution to a new era of human progress.

Europe is situated at the intersection of the two axes, East-West and North-South, in a unique position for better or worse. I have already noted that, in certain respects, this is a delicate position that might, however, become very important. Europe's central position and its peculiar characteristics ought to allow it to play a significant role and to influence the course of events in a positive way. However, Europe must want to do this, and prepare itself seriously to meet the challenge; above all, Europe must achieve effective unity — first as a true economic community, and later as a unified political entity.

Europe is compelled to follow this path, principally in its own interest. "What we can already say about today's Europe, is that if we Europeans decide to do nothing or to do very little about it, we are, in fact, taking a vitally important no-decision about our future, laying the groundwork for tragic situations of economic dependence, unemployment, and social tension."* But, in a crisis as serious as the present one, Europe also has moral and political obligations to the world as a whole. Under these circumstances, those who can act, must do so. And, if Europe fails in this respect, and does not do all that is in its power to improve the human condition, it will have to answer one day to the judgment of history.

The political imperative to bring order to the East-West and North-South axes of the human system, which I have just sketched, may appear to be a Utopian prescription for a brave new world — for a world that will never be because the present one cannot change. This is a criticism that must be rejected categorically. I am fully aware of the difficulty of bringing about these transformations and even more of making them work. But, after much thought and long discussion, I have become convinced that such designs — however vague, idealistic, and impossible they may seem

---

* Andre Danzin, *Science and the Renaissance of Europe* (New York: Pergamon Press, 1979).

today — have a reasonable chance of becoming the reality of the world of tomorrow. Given the present state of affairs, to have the courage of Utopia is the only way to be truly realistic. *Realpolitik has become obsolete — we need a new Realutopie.**

---

* A word invented by the late German philosopher Ernst Bloch.

THE GREAT HIDDEN RESOURCE

Learning to Create the Future

The third basic requirement is to learn to govern the huge conglomeration of societies and systems, ever more complex and overlapping, that constitute our world. However, in order to learn to govern the world, we must first learn to govern ourselves. That is a primary requirement, which, as I have already pointed out a number of times, demands a sweeping cultural evolution. Thus the most urgent imperative is *to promote the development of the human individual*, without which no other development, no policy, no future project is possible, and without which humanity will be incapable of stopping itself in its race towards the precipice. I will now try to draw some conclusions.

What is called "progress" has become such a frantic upheaval — so mechanistic and artificial, so inexorable and unpredictable — that we are no longer able to control it, or even to understand its significance. Our situation is literally dramatic. A widening *chasm* separates us from the real world, once familiar but now alien. At the same time, a *failing* in ourselves prevents us from distinguishing between things that worsen our position and those that might improve it. As a result, we become panic-stricken and act in a thoughtless manner. Our situation would soon become desperate if there were not *a final safety resort in the depths of our being.* This is the innate richness of understanding, vision, and creativity which is the heritage of each individual and yet remains forgotten and unexploited. It is accompanied by resources of moral energy not yet tapped, and still available to us. The choice between being and not being, between surviving or going under — or, rather, between surviving in a manner worthy of our humanity or sinking to sub-human levels —depends almost exclusively on our ability to mobilize and develop this hidden natural potential within us.

Even a superficial glance confirms that the modern human being is unfinished. We have had spectacular successes and have carried our knowledge, power, and influence to unheard-of heights, but we have been fooling ourselves by believing that we have forever attained the era of affluence and well-being, and need not undergo the inconvenience or effort of adjusting to the transformations we are causing around us. As a result, we have remained underdeveloped, lagging behind the realities that have grown beyond us. The only way to recoup and to catch up with them is to concentrate our capacities on developing ourselves as may be required, that is to say, by *learning to live in consonance with the new, fantastic, half-artificial world of our own creation.*

What we are called upon to do is the equivalent of making a radical change from one cultural epoch to another — to emerge from the past into the present, and to continue without pause into the future. Even if there are some common denominators, the required evolution will be different for the citizens of different parts of the world, which makes the process even more complex. Nothing like it has ever before been tried in the past, for in fact it has never been necessary. It is the extraordinary circumstances of the present that oblige us to undertake a task of such difficulty and scope; but, on the other hand, we possess unprecedented means, which ought to allow us to confront this change as an exceptional but acceptable challenge.

In order to prepare ourselves and become actors worthy of this new phase in the human adventure, countless initiatives will be necessary at all levels, in all parts of the world. Participation in the effort must be assured from society's main centers of interpersonal communication — families, schools, churches, towns and villages, businesses, trade unions, factories, international organizations, mass media, youth groups, political parties, sports associations, etc. The main thing is to begin, and to begin well.

With this end in view, The Club of Rome and its friends have thought out a series of activities to be developed. I will describe them briefly in the hope that some readers will help by making their own contributions in support of these activities, or by offering constructive criticisms. Three specific objectives have been selected:

- Creation of a movement of innovative learning on the broadest possible bases;
- Promotion of the development of alternative projects for the future by mobilizing the creativity of the young; and
- Stimulation of a fundamental renewal in our current way of thinking.

A project based on innovative learning was sponsored by The Club of Rome in 1976 as the forerunner of a cluster of other projects or research studies to be undertaken in subsequent years. This initial project culminated in a report published in 1979, the title of which — *No Limits to Learning: Bridging the Human Gap** — gives an idea of its inspiring concept and goal. It is known in short as the Learning Project, a name that summarizes a vital necessity that I hope will be recognized by all those who have the future at heart.

It is paradoxical that, with all our knowledge about so many things, we should know almost nothing of how we learn, and how the unknown and invisible mental mechanisms that control our learning can be improved. One thing that is known, incidentally, is that the average brain capacity of the individual is far greater than that which is normally called into use; and also that the human brain can probably be stimulated to improve its intellectual and existential performance. We also know that learning must involve the whole person; and, for learning to be most effective, the natural, psycho-physical conditions of the organism must not be impaired by deficiencies in food or health. Particularly important are the periods of prenatal development, infancy, and early childhood, and the "cultural" exchanges between mother and child and among children. To discuss all that, however, would lead us too far from our subject.

Learning depends on processes and goals that are too complex to be ascribed simply to education. It goes without saying that the latter is an essential component and an irreplaceable instrument of learning and human formation

---

* James W. Botkin, Mahdi Elmandjra, and Mircea Malitza, *No Limits to Learning: Bridging the Human Gap* (New York: Pergamon Press, 1979).

in general. The tradition of education is, however, rather conservative and educators are ill at ease when innovation is required. Education is usually anchored in the past, provided by parents for children, conveyed by teacher to pupil, transmitted from the initiated to the novice. Learning, on the contrary, generally arises spontaneously and has no predetermined rules; it is more within the reach of the young than of adults. The latter, who often have greater need of learning, are sometimes impervious to its benefits — especially when they wield power.

In learning, manual labor and group activities are essential. The aim is not merely for the individual to become literate and educated. It is also to gain an understanding and tolerance of others; to re-establish the value of communion with Nature and the transcendent; to assign the future at least as high a priority as the present; to find one's way amid complexities and to reduce them to simple, comprehensive terms; to adapt to uncommon dimensions, to super-speeds, to rapid changes; and to acquire some of the cultural horizons I have mentioned in the preceding pages. This set of things to be learned is certainly indispensable for an improved quality of life and probably also for survival. And we must be convinced that, when all is said and done, everything depends on the quality of the individual, which in turn depends to a large extent on his ability to learn to be and to become. These reflections lead us finally to the very heart of the human problematique.

The cited report demonstrates, as one might imagine, that in a mass society in rapid transformation *learning must be based on participation and anticipation*. This is a requirement that reflects two aspects of the human solidarity that is the very essence of a mature and responsible society — the first related to the present, the second to the future. The report underlines that collectivities and societies, too, must learn — they must learn to fulfill their functions and to evolve in a more proficient way in this new world; and their learning cannot be merely the sum total of individual learning.

On close examination, however, this document reveals nothing that was not already known. The stimulating ideas it presents were already in existence somewhere. Yet the fact that the report presents them in an understandable form at an opportune moment is important.* This fact alone ought to help awaken the consciousness of reluctant decision-makers and stir up sluggish public opinion to the discovery of a most precious possession which they have never considered. Along with solar energy, human capacities — constantly neglected and wasted, even stifled for fear they might be translated into radical socio-political ideas — are the greatest resource at the disposal of humankind. They are a resource that is not only eminently renewable, but also one that can expand with time; and they are the only resource that can help us find a way out of the present predicament. To leave such a resource in its present state of abandon is therefore dangerously stupid and wasteful, even suicidal.

In order to strengthen this growing awareness, the initial effort must be extended in several directions. Conscious of this necessity, UNESCO is ready to employ the means at its disposal to orient its institutional programs towards *learning* in the 'eighties. To this end, it is now studying, along with The Club of Rome, ways of undertaking a number of research efforts and pilot projects. Two of the activities

---

* This was also true of the first report to The Club of Rome, *The Limits to Growth.*

under consideration can be pointed out here:

• The first is an international project, to be developed over several years, for neurophysiological, socio-psychological, and pedagogical research on the processes that govern our learning, and the ways in which they can be improved. This is a project of wide scope, which should be supported by UNESCO and other international organizations and backed up by satellite national programs, but which should be carried out exclusively in scientific circles, away from bureaucracy. The results should permit human-kind to emerge more rapidly from its present condition of inferiority and to learn what it takes to attain a higher plateau of evolution and performance.

• The second is a series of pilot projects in selected villages of the Third World, which would be transformed into self-administering communities for rural develop-ment. The element of innovation would consist in the establishment in each village of volunteer nuclei for agri-cultural development, health, and education, which would be guided by "barefoot" agronomists, doctors, and educators, serving a large number of villages. Other forms of simple assistance could help this experiment in inte-grated local development get under way; and, if enough villages passed the test, application of the concept on a larger scale would be considered. I need not stress how important it is that this initiative should succeed. Half the world's population are peasants in the Third World. They should not have to leave their own soil; they should be able to learn how to live there decently.

The ministries of education in many countries — includ-ing France, Austria, Spain, and soon several nations of the

Third World — are also studying a number of projects that they themselves can carry out with the collaboration of a body of teachers. In Venezuela, for example, the Ministry for the Development of Human Intelligence has instituted some very interesting programs for the development of intellectual capacity in widely differing situations — among school children, families, military recruits, civil servants, and citizens from various regions of the country. One of these programs, called "learning to think," has just started and will soon be expanded to include 40,000 teachers and more than a million pupils between the ages of 9 and 12. China is following these experiments closely and has just created a special organization to apply the Venezuelan methods to pilot projects on a scale proportionate to her own dimensions.

The American Postage Stamp That Says it All

USA
Learning never ends

Dr. Aurelio Peccei
President, The Club of Rome
via Giorgione, 163
00147 Rome, Italy

FRANKLIN, MA
SEP
2
1980
02038

FIRST DAY OF ISSUE

It is still too early to speak of conclusive results, but already one can perceive how *learning is destined to become a cardinal concept in a world that is groping in semi-darkness, searching for means of salvation.* In a few years' time, it will be possible to assess the progress that has been achieved. Meanwhile, all those wishing to make their contribution to this undertaking will certainly find a way to do so. It is gratifying that even the American postal service has embarked on this path. In 1980, it introduced the stamp reproduced on page 174, bearing the very appropriate motto "Learning Never Ends" — which tells us the way we must travel.

The Pure Source of Youth

Finally, what future shall we invent? There would be no sense in inventing a purely imaginary future. What we must envisage is not just a future worth living, but one that can actually can be achieved — one that we can effectively hope to build. It is much easier, however, to judge, even at a glance, which futures are not possible, or to decide immediately which we would never want to see, than to define futures that are both feasible and desirable.

In my opinion, the true goal of the human adventure is to succeed in creating a world in which the best of human qualities can flourish in a climate of mutual understanding and union with Nature. Others will certainly have different views. And I am not sure that everyone is really interested in seeing, or in bequeathing to posterity, a future that is better than the present if this entails sacrifices now.

One might even assert the contrary. One has only to consider the allegedly objective projections of certain demographers, economists, or technologists, which have what one might almost call sadistic overtones. They foresee an automated, science fiction world of robots, in which machines would construct other machines, which would in turn set still others in motion, without any need for human beings. Those whom one might call "the high priests" of the atom, of computers, of manipulated genes, of information science, of artificial intelligence, would supervise the mass of citizens, checking that their needs were satisfied and their well-being assured. To defend this new world, there would be supreme and splendid weapons, obviously designed for cosmic warfare since they would not be usable on Earth.

This world of the future would be inhabited by 10 to 12 billion people, or more, living partly under the sea or on satellites. Plants and vegetables with an economic value would be cultivated, and useful animals domesticated; the others would be relegated to special reserves. We do not know yet what would be done with insects and microbes. Wildlife, which is the torch of life itself, would be preserved, if not in its pristine state, then as far as possible in air-conditioned laboratories. Other research centers would have the task of creating new forms of life for greater human benefit and glory. Social justice would be ensured through uniformity; the hours and modes of work and the use of leisure time would be well regulated; and freedom of movement, access to green areas, and the right to education and culture would be rationally allocated in accordance with models worked out in advance by highly sophisticated computers.

I believe, though, that such an ant-heap world will never exist. If it existed, its inhabitants would hate it even if they could eat their fill and exist in relative comfort. They would have lost forever their marvellous natural environment, which would be replaced by an inanimate, artificial, and robot-filled milieu in which all well-being would be merely illusory. A surfeit of mechanical and electronic equipment, servo-mechanisms, automated devices, and telecommunications gadgets would diminish their contacts with each other. Similarly, the reduction of manual labor to a minimum would eliminate their contact with materials that can be shaped into beautiful or useful forms, and would deprive them of the satisfaction of performing a socially useful task. They would feel that a part of their humanity had been taken away from them.

I reject this scenario. But what other can I suggest? Or, more generally, *what alternative "desirable" scenarios can be imagined that might be feasible* — for example, for the year 2000 and beyond? Even if scenarios for the future are in fashion today, the technique of their preparation in clear and rational form is very complicated and has not yet been convincingly mastered. Besides, a scenario is only the beginning. In relation to projects for the future that are to be implemented, it is only a rough sketch, a very general indication of an ensemble of interacting situations, policies, and behaviors which may represent the coherent reality of tomorrow, a goal to be pursued but whose feasibility remains unproved.

Still, this new world of tomorrow, towards which we would like humanity to steer its course, must be imagined, defined, and designed in its broad outlines. At the moment, we say half in jest that we don't know where we're headed but we're going there anyway — backwards and at full speed. Tomorrow we ought to know somewhat better where we want to go and to find the most appropriate ways and means to arrive there in an orderly fashion, and also to understand what sacrifices we must make to reach our objective.

Let us see whether it is possible to explore this terrain a little further. According to current claims — and this time there is no joke about it — the major decisions are being made by a world that is white, affluent, and male. There is both sarcasm and protest in that assertion, because those who do not belong to the white race, and are not wealthy, cannot share fully in the great human decisions, and because women have little voice in such matters. One may add that this world is also one of *adults;* it is they who guide our affairs. The young are excluded from the game. They are not consulted, not even when the decisions affect the long-term future, which they and not the adults will experience.

And yet, the young make up the great majority of the world's population — 36 percent of which is under age 15 and nearly 60 percent under 30. Thus *even reasons of justice and democracy demand that the voices of youth should be heard*, especially on all questions involving the distant future. Other reasons, incidentally, support this argument. The young have a greater stake in the future, and also possess the flexibility needed for self-renewal in a world that is changing before our eyes. They have their whole lives in front of them to put new ideas into practice. They are more critical of contemporary society and, not yet being enmeshed in it, are more free to use their creative powers to imagine a different one. And they are more pure in heart — hence more sensitive to the need to create a more just, more honest, and more humane world. They can be the true bearers of a new concept of civilization.

On the other hand, adults have so far shown themselves to be less willing to make a serious commitment to the creation of the future. The idea of offering this possibility to selected groups of young people thus was born. I have been talking about it now for three or four years to friends in various places, and have found them as enthusiastic about the idea itself as they are skeptical about the possibility of putting it into practice. Nevertheless, the project, which has come to be called *Forum Humanum*, has begun to take shape.

Its fundamental aim is to make all of us aware of *what "other futures" are possible*, and what must be done to make them more likely to happen. That the task of opening the debate on this crucial theme should be delegated to the young should not be surprising. From what I have just said, it appears that they are better suited for it than their elders. And probably only a generational change can bring about the sweeping cultural evolution that humanity needs to make a new departure. It is perhaps not a mere coincidence that, in other species as well, evolution occurs from one generation to the next, with the young as its prime actors. In these species, evolution is biological, and the genetic code that governs it is transmitted at the time of procreation — which is a function of youth.

After a thorough discussion of the main concept of Forum Humanum, a group of first-class young men and women of several nationalities declared that this is a promising venture in the service of humankind, and they therefore chose to commit themselves to it. This initial group is prepared to expand, by co-opting other young people in their twenties or early thirties from different parts of the world.

The design of the project is simple and bold. It will start with *the creation of a network of centers for research, study, debate, and proposals on the human future, directed exclusively by young people.* In order to involve a varied spectrum of cultures and points of view, these centers will be based in a number of different countries. Their purpose will be to examine alternatives for world society as it can, realistically be envisaged — say, for the year 2000 and beyond —and the policies, strategies, and means that will have to be employed to that end. These studies will be eminently interdisciplinary, and will deal with all important aspects of the life of society — from values to political institutions, from the use of resources to relationships with Nature, from the human habitat to human rights and responsibilities, from economics to education, from social justice to security and the quality of life. The plan is to complete the project by 1985, which has been designated the United Nations Youth Year.

For this endeavor to succeed, however, there must be a reasonable assurance of financial support. A fairly large amount of money will, in fact, be required, especially to maintain centers in less developed countries and to operate a small secretariat located at a strategic point in the network, as well as to enable the participants to meet frequently in one center or another — to get to know each other, to compare their ideas, to judge their respective progress, and to blend their efforts into a coherent whole. This financial problem has not yet been solved. Experience shows how frustrating and humiliating, particularly when dealing with young people, it is to see good purposes and logical requirements thwarted by lack of financial support. Forum Humanum is a case in point. That is why activities have started at a slower pace than initially desired. Four meetings have so far been scheduled for 1981, from April to November, in Rome, Caracas, Salzburg (Austria) and Santander (Spain). A prospectus will then be readied to launch an international fund-raising campaign.

This plea for the young does not mean that adults should not participate in the Forum Humanum. On the contrary, a number of them, including myself, have already volunteered to assist the young people in their efforts, and all such offers are welcome. It does not mean either that the adults should abdicate their present position of authority — which, incidentally, they appear to have no intention of doing. The issue is quite different; it concerns not *who* makes the decisions, but *how* they are made, how power in human society should henceforth be exercised.

To guide the multi-billion human family towards constructive, not destructive, ends will be a tremendous challenge. National policies and behavior must be inspired by a clear understanding of realities, a keen sense of global issues, a responsibility to the future, and a consciousness of the species. All these qualities, alas, do not exist today. The young should instil them in us, show how salutary they are, how immensely profitable their cost/benefit ratio can be for all of us.

Once this spadework is done, it is logical that groups of citizens as large as possible, indeed the whole of society, be involved in the construction of desired futures. The contribution of each and every individual will be required, and all will benefit from the results.

Let me conclude by saying that, if we look well ahead into possible futures, we will learn many lessons. For one thing, we will discover to what an incredible extent our present modes of thinking and acting are wrong or inadequate. To invent a better future will thus require us to improve ourselves and our behavior first. For another, we will perceive at a glance that, at a time of metamorphic change such as this, innovation is indispensable. And, as a consequence, we will understand how politically wise it will be to enhance the art of governance *by making adequate room for the imagination and aspirations of the younger generations.*

The Human Revolution

Nothing could be more obvious than the need for solid conceptual groundwork to support the complex of innovative policies and activities which are required to translate the ideals and perspectives we have been discussing into concrete reality. It is evident that our current ways of thinking reflect ideologies and experiences of a past very different from the present. A wide gap has thus opened between the beliefs, values, principles, norms, frames of reference, and mental attitudes that we normally employ as guides, and those that are now necessary in view of the nature and extent of the challenges of our age. This is a grave handicap, indeed.

Furthermore, to fulfill our tremendous responsibilites, *we all, as modern men and women, must recover our humanity.* We have lost it to a great extent in a frantic race for "progress." Our religious inspiration has appreciably declined, for it was born of the great mysteries of Nature and the Universe, and these have now been largely resolved by the exact sciences. Our spirituality has suffered severe blows, but how could this be otherwise when we discover that all we know, from inert matter to living beings, is nothing but energy in different forms and combinations? Harmonizing energy and spirituality is no easy task, nor is it easy to reconcile science and religion. Spirituality and religion cannot be rationalized, any more than one can readily imagine energy or science having a soul.

Modern human beings are absorbed by hopes, aspirations, and tasks which are all focused on the material sphere. The very nature of the present-day world imposes such choices upon them; they have no alternatives. Everything that is not quantifiable, measurable, or expressible in terms of money, or that cannot be transformed into data, represented by a graph, translated into an image, or put on a screen, has little or no value. The intangible lies outside the circle of things that count. I have no time for an analysis of the decline in non-material values. I would simply like to point out that the model of the modern man or woman to which we seem to aspire is someone who has command over tangible things and who understands machines, gadgets, and computers, who lives and works in an air-conditioned, artificially-lighted building, and who drives a high-powered car through hair-raising traffic to make contact with other machines or gadgets, to dialogue with other computers, or to disappear into other science-fiction buildings; or who finally jumps on a plane or into another car, with the ultimate goal of reaching a color television set and a well-stocked refrigerator.

These ideal male and female types attach more importance to the artificial world they have created, or are tempted to create, than to the natural world that has created them. They are primarily interested in the things they manufacture themselves, or that they drive, manipulate, or manage. This applies even to food, which they prefer tinned, frozen, bottled, processed, and preserved. Nature occupies a distant second place, and metaphysics have no attraction for them. Not even their fellow beings are worth considering. They are stereotyped, almost faceless, and there are so many of them that they have become numbers rather than persons. To communicate with them is difficult, uninteresting; besides, they are all too busy doing other things to listen. So everyone remains isolated, even if each individual has a good deal of power, possesses some wealth, and can operate various types of equipment. Thus they all feel a void growing within, and would like to bring order to their lives, to give greater meaning to what they are and what they are doing. They would also like to have warmer human contacts. But all that is impossible because their present mode of being is faulty; and it is faulty because their way of thinking is inadequate, and cannot serve the purposes to which they aspire.

A basically new way of thinking is indispensable — thinking capable of saving the mass of humankind of the technological age from its increasing aridity, and of making each of us a full-fledged human being willing to face up to the challenges before us and to fulfill the role that is ours by reason of our position of power and responsibility in the world. This way of thinking must be eminently humanistic. *Only a new humanism can bring about this near-miracle*, and accomplish the renaissance of the human spirit.

This humanism consonant with our epoch must replace and reverse principles and norms that we have heretofore regarded as untouchable, but that have become inapplicable, or discordant with our purpose; it must encourage the rise of new value systems to redress our inner balance, and of new spiritual, ethical, philosophical, social, political, esthetic, and artistic motivations to fill the emptiness of our life; it must be capable of restoring within us — as our most precious possession and need — love, friendship, understanding, solidarity, a spirit of sacrifice, conviviality; and it must make us understand that the more closely these qualities link us to other forms of life, and to our brothers and sisters everywhere in the world, the more we shall gain.

This new humanism must also be sufficiently strong and flexible to allow us to assert control over the material revolutions that now dominate us; to show us how to encourage, and give peaceful and constructive direction to, the socio-political revolution now under way in human systems, which at present we can only allow to smoulder or explode into violence; and to make us realize that never again, whatever the cost, must we renounce the primacy of the spirit. Moreover, it must be of universal scope, and exert such influence that it will not only change the views and behavior of certain nations, or of certain classes of citizens, but also be accepted by the mass of the world's population as something of their own. Finally, it must allow our species to justify its exalted place on Earth as that of an innovative, moderating, and protective element in the flux of life, not as an absolute arbiter with self-arrogated rights of life and death over all other species.

This new humanism therefore must itself be revolutionary and have its ethical and moral foundations in the human conscience. It must be *a truly human revolution*. Its success is the very condition of survival for humankind in the difficult times to come. And the achievement of that success is the challenge that modern men and women must accept.

There is no doubt that the undertaking will be long, painful, agonizing, and controversial. Yet, in spite of the disasters and the darkness that threatened the world, there are signs that the seeds of change may perhaps already have begun to germinate. These signs tell us that *it is not impossible to pursue the human revolution* — on the condition that the most sensitive, imaginative, and creative sectors of society manage to unite in order to galvanize into action those elements that are still hesitant and scattered. In all humility, in order to stimulate discussion and criticism, I will offer at the end of this book a few seeds of the wisdom which, in my opinion, ought to inspire the new humanism.

At the dawn of this decisive decade of the 'eighties, therefore, we must not despair. We, the citizens of the world, can still take the future into our own hands and begin to forge our common destiny together. In conclusion, at the risk of repeating myself, I wish to emphasize once more that, among the thousands of things that must be done, three are of fundamental importance. I have briefly illustrated them in the last part of this volume. They can be summarized in inverse order, so as to start from the cornerstone of our future. They are:

1. *The human revolution* that places the individual at the center of all development and must raise the human quality, capacity, and sense of responsibility.
In a strict sense, it consists in:
• the ethical, philosophical, and humanistic renewal of universal thought.
In a broader sense, it also includes other cultural developments, which must facilitate, accompany, and give practical impetus to the new humanism. I have mentioned two of vast scope:
• the design of preferred alternative futures, prepared by young people who are ready to commit themselves to their achievement; and
• a movement for innovative learning with a broad popular base, extending throughout the world.

2. *The politico-structural evolution of society*, and of

human systems, to assure their governability.

Two cardinal elements of this undertaking are:

• the transformation of East-West tensions into active collaboration; and

• the self-restructuring of the South so that it can be integrated organically into the world system.

3. *The adoption of global policies and strategies* by means of voluntary coalitions of nations, established without waiting for systematic or generalized plans.

There will soon be an opportunity to demonstrate, by an act of leadership, the quality of existing political will in this sense:

• the North-South summits — to start with the first in the autumn of 1981 — which should set the world on the path of new forms of future global collaboration.

The generations whose destiny it is to live in this crucial period of history can no longer remain in ignorance of the predicament of humankind, nor of the kind of future they will have, for better or worse, according to the choices they make and the courses of action they adopt. If the collective action of all peoples and nations is intelligent and responsible, the finest hour of the human adventure still lies ahead of us.

For the decisions of the 'eighties to move in this direction, however, someone must take the initiative, and must call on others to discuss these issues from a long-term global perspective.

It is my sincere hope is that this brief book may contribute to that goal.

Seeds of Wisdom?

- Although procreation is the supreme form of human expression, it must respond to a strict social ethic.
- When the choice is between terminating pregnancy, or conceiving children who probably will be destined to a life of misery or death through starvation or war, no one could impose the second alternative.
- In a world in which overpopulation is creating planetary problems, national demographic policies must be compatible with the general interests of humankind.
- The quality of the population is more important than its quantity, and it alone can offset the effects of the population explosion.
- Populations must be capable of solving the problems they create.
- The individual cannot be equated with his basic needs; being a rational, spiritual and artistic creature, with a taste for dreams, creativity, and pleasure, he has many other needs and wants.
- Generally speaking, the only needs that can be defined as such are those that can reasonably be satisfied, individually or collectively.
- The conservation of Nature and respect for other forms of life are an essential condition both for the quality and preservation of human life.
- The protection of human cultural heritage through the world is equally essential.
- There can be no exclusive rights over the natural resources of the world; they must be preserved and shared as equitably as possible, whatever their geographical location.
- The same principle applies to the information,

knowledge, and know-how necessary for human progress and well-being, whoever may have proprietary rights over them.

• It is the duty of every generation to leave a better world to its successors.

• Our responsibilities and obligations to our descendants and to other forms of life increase with the growth of our knowledge and power.

• The consciousness of the species must take precedence over class or national consciousness.

• Only the prior acceptance of human duties and responsibilities can justify the proclamation of human rights.

• New "social contracts" must establish the "social minima" of guarantees and services that constitute the rights of the citizen and the obligations of society; and, conversely, they must establish the duties of the citizen and the rights of society.

• Certain ceilings of "social maxima" must also be established as a natural corollary to the "social minima."

• The principle of territorial sovereignty is an insurmountable obstacle to peace. It must gradually be limited and reformed, and finally abandoned; and it is up to the most powerful nations to set an example in this regard.

• An appropriate variety of supranational, subnational, transnational and a-national solutions is indispensable for the progressive development of a world community.

• An intermediate stage might be the formation of regional or subregional groupings, federations, or communities, which would at the same time safeguard local autonomy.

• The "new order" must not be "international" or merely "economic," but as far as possible "global" in the full sense; and it must establish the rules of coherence and the rights and duties of the world community.

- Security is a primary need that cannot be guaranteed by armaments but only by the cultural maturity of individuals and societies.
- Social justice and solidarity within the world community are essential to achieve healthier and more viable societies.
- Self-reliant development of the poorest regions, with the full cooperation of other regions, must be a priority of the world community.
- It is essential to recognize the intrinsic interdependence of economics and ecology.
- The progressive scarcity of physical resources demands their optimum use in the interests of harmonious global development.
- Our economic concepts must evolve to take adequate account of the utilization value of goods and services, and to allow the conservation of all available natural resources.
- The ethic of moderation must replace the myth of overconsumption.
- The objective and logic of dynamic equilibrium in human systems must replace the objective and logic of growth.
- Since the efficiency of some external self-regulating systems has weakened, self-regulation must be developed in human systems.
- A minimum of consistency in the aims and activities of the various societies being indispensable in the world context, global medium- and long-term methods of consultation and planning must be devised to guarantee maximum local and regional autonomy.
- The respective roles of planning, private enterprise, and public initiative in the economy must be reviewed and coordinated.
- The growing complexity of human systems demands competent and effective management at all levels, from

the local to the global.

- The techno-scientific enterprise must be radically reoriented in order to serve the whole human race instead of sectoral interests.
- Human development, in the fullest sense, is the supreme goal of humankind, and as such must have absolute priority over every other development or goal.
- Human development must be anticipatory, to prepare people in advance, and is thus distinguished from genetic evolution, which takes place through reaction and adaptation.
- Spiritual, ethico-moral, socio-political, and cultural virtues and values are foundations of the new society to be built.
- Education, research, reflection, and learning are the instruments of its development; they must promote a spirit of participation, anticipation, solidarity, and universality.

Aurelio Peccei

Aurelio Peccei was born in Turin, Italy in 1908. He earned his doctorate in economics in 1930 and his early years as a scholar provided the focus for much of his later thinking. As a multi-talented young manager with Fiat, Peccei was sent to China, where he remained until 1938. Upon his return to Italy, he immediately became involved in the anti-fascist front and later joined the freedom fighters of the Italian Resistance. In 1944 he was arrested and condemned, for nearly a year, to a fascist prison.

The liberation and the subsequent rebuilding of Europe afforded Aurelio Peccei many new opportunities. After several years of work in the senior management of Fiat in Italy, he was assigned to represent the company in Latin America. In Argentina, he successfully established factories throughout the country, all the while sharpening his awareness and concern for the global human condition and the intricacies of human problems.

Peccei's travels and work in the developing nations of the world led him to seek more effective methods of economic assistance. At his urging, Italconsult, a non-profit international engineering and economic consulting unit, was organized, with Peccei as managing director. In 1964, Peccei assumed the direction of Olivetti during a period of difficulty within the corporation. Four years later, with a small circle of other concerned individuals, he founded The Club of Rome and remains its President today. In addition, Aurelio Peccei is the author of several books, numerous published articles, and he has lectured throughout the world.

. . . and the End?

Humanity has found a scientific method of putting an end to its career.

Hiroshima 1945

The atomic bomb which destroyed Hiroshima in 1945 had a destructive force equivalent to 15 kilotons.

Today's strategic and tactical nuclear weapons, which are widely dispersed over the globe, number over 50,000 and have a total destructive capability estimated at 15,000,000 kilotons. These weapons are more than ample to destroy every city in the world several times over.

Reproduced with permission from the publication *World Military and Social Expenditures 1980,* by Ruth Leger Sivard, World Priorities, Leesburg, Virginia, 22075, USA.